BEST WAY TO TEACH YOUR CHILD TO READ
Teach your child to read and write using stories, play and movement.

Written and illustrated by Paul Mackie.
Cover Picture graphics: - Pixabay

Library and Archives Canada Cataloguing in Publication

Mackie, Paul - Author
BEST WAY TO TEACH YOUR CHILD TO READ

ISBN 978-1-988986-18-0

Contact author: educationalchildsplay@gmail.com

Author's website: http://howtoteachchildrentoread.ca

Contents

Contents

BUILDING SELF ESTEEM IN CHILDREN

- Treat children with respect and always talk to them at their level.
- Encourage and focus on a child's interests and strengths.
- Have expectations that are age appropriate.
- Show children they are appreciated and loved.
- Give lots of praise, even for the small day to day things.
- Be gentle and reasonable.
- Firm-discipline is not punishment, but guidance.
- Model the behavior you expect from children through understanding and communication.
- Let children know your expectations and consequences.
- If you give a consequence for an action, then always follow through.
- Use positive reinforcement to reward proper behavior.
- Give children choices.
- Be consistent, remain calm, state expectations and consequences for actions; and always follow through with what you have said.

DEDICATION

This book is dedicated to giving pre and early grade school children the skills they need to learn how to read, write and be the best that they can be.

THIS BOOK IS FOR: Parents, pre-school teachers, Early Childhood Educators, Day Cares, anyone wanting to help children to be the best they can be.

WHAT YOU NEED TO KNOW ABOUT THIS BOOK
This book presents four ways to teach children how to read:
1. Reading stories to your child.
2. Play-based activities.
3. Developmental movements.
4. Phonics and pre-primer sight words.

The book has four sections:
1. A way to Teach Reading and Writing
2. Grade School Learning to Read.
3. Preschool Learning To Read.
4. Children Having Difficulties Reading.

The Reading Environment – Setting up a home or teaching environment is critical to help children learn how to read.

Play based activities - That scientists are saying children need in the first seven years of their developmental life.

Developmental Movements – Called "Move and Improve" are the same movements as in the developmental stories in this book, but in adult form.

This book combines elements and pages from my other books; A Walk In The Jungle; Gordy Visits The Mountains; Educational Child's Play; Play-Based Ways To Teach Your Child To Read and Fast Start For Early Readers Kindergarten.

For Those That Want To Know More - This section of the book explains the benefits and how to do the book's activities in more depth.

The storybook movements are demonstrated here:
https://howtoteachchildrentoread.ca/

Questions - contact the author: educationalchildsplay@gmail.com

DISCLAIMER

THIS BOOK: "Best Way To Teach Your Child To Read" is designed to help children gain the physical and other skills needed when learning to read and write; this book does provide a method showing how to teach children the basics needed when learning to read and write; the authors book "Fast Start For Early Readers-Kindergarten" explains the learning to read method in greater depth.

Note: Always consult a doctor before beginning any exercise program. The author offers the information and movements in this book only when advised by a doctor to do so and does not accept any responsibility for the information's misuse.

The suggested movements are combinations and adaptations of several programs, methods and techniques that the author has practiced for many years, but in no way do they represent the potential, methods or techniques of those programs.

The author's claims are based on benefits to himself and of children in his care; the activity benefits listed may help with but are not guaranteed or proven results.

AGE APPROPRIATNESS
The activities in this book are for children from birth to grade school; as well as having the same potential benefits for adult caregivers or teachers.

THE DEVELOPMENTAL STORIES are generally for children aged 2 years or older but can be read to younger children; if younger children will allow it. The activity movements can be done hand over hand by the caregiver for the child.

The methods presented in this book are intended to help children develop the skills needed to learn how to read and write but are not a guarantee of success that a child will learn how to read or write.

All methods in this book are the adapted ideas of the author and do not represent the views of other books, authors and their methods.

WHAT CAN THIS BOOK DO FOR A CHILD'S READING?

This book introduces you to movement and play-based ways to help children develop the physical and other skills to learn how to read and write.

The methods used in this book are Phonics; pre-primer sight words; developmental movements; the Balance Board; telling stories; and crossing the body's midline when reading or writing.

The activities in this book are a series of developmental movements and fun activities. It is hoped that the activities will develop a child's cognitive, behavioral, emotional, reading, writing and motor skills.

Unfortunately, there are no guarantees; the possible outcomes are based on the author's own experiences and observed results of children in the author's care; it is hoped that you can achieve the same outcomes.
I can safely say that the information and methods in this book helped me, other adults, and children in my care; they got me through my working life in many different careers; my hope is they work for you as they did for myself and others.

POSSIBLE OUTCOMES FOR CHILDREN

- Learn how to read and write.
- Increase ability to problem solve.
- Socialize and get to know each other.
- Increase social skills, confidence and cooperation.
- Learn how to handle stress and emotions.
- Increase communication and thinking skills.
- Participate in group activities.
- Increase self-direction.
- Enhanced ability to sequence information.
- Increase motivation.
- Develop the Brain's neural pathways.
- Increase organizational skills.
- Greater sense of rhythm and balance.
- Increased enthusiasm to learn.
- Improved coordination.
- Increase emotional self-control and self-esteem.
- Increase visual and auditory processing.
- Cross the midline of the body for reading and writing.

A WAY TO TEACH READING AND WRITING

SIDEWAYS 8 - LEFT-RIGHT-AND CURSIVE ALPHABET WRITING

SIDEWAYS 8

LEFT ALPHABET

RIGHT ALPHABET

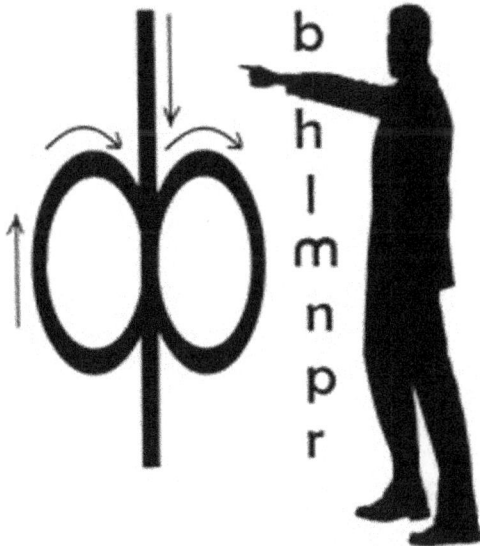

CURSIVE ALPHABET

All children learn and develop at different rates and ages, so you may have to adapt the activities in this book to suit your child's abilities.

DO THESE MOVEMENTS BEFORE YOU START

The Author recommends doing 4 easy to do movements before starting any activity; they are: WATER, ENERGY BOOST, CROSSOVERS and CONNECTIONS.

WATER

helps with: Oxygenating the brain.

Why it is useful: Water helps conduct the electrical and chemical processes of the brain for clear thinking; computer work; operating machinery; and organizational activities.

How it is done: Having a water bottle close by is an easy way to take a drink during the work day.

ENERGY BOOST

Helps with: Increased energy and relaxation.

Why it is useful: An energy boost when needed keeps you alert and energized during the work day; for paying attention to details; and filling out paperwork.

How it is done: Place your hand on your neck (palm on the Adam's apple) with thumb on one side and fingers on the other. Move your hand down until you feel your collar-bone, jump over it and Massage the soft spots between the next set of ribs and the collarbone. Place your other hand on your belly button (do not massage with this hand). Switch both hands and repeat for about 30 seconds.

CROSSOVERS

Is said to help with: Accessing the whole brain.

Why it is useful: Using both sides of the brain is essential, for reading; writing; creativity; comprehension; body coordination; public speaking; and stress reduction.

How it is done: Lift your left leg and touch your left knee with your right hand. Put the foot down and lift your right leg and touch your right knee with your left hand. Repeat 3x.

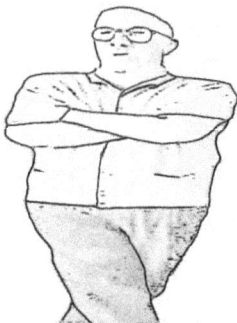

CONNECTIONS

Is said to help with: De-stressing and focusing on problems.

Why it is useful: Being relaxed and focused helps make your work day easier; improves self-esteem; leading meetings; seeing others point of view; and multi-tasking.

How it is done: Stand up straight, sit or lie on the floor, cross your feet at the ankles, and give yourself a big hug by placing your hands under each arm pit; can be done standing, sitting or lying down.

See pages 27 - 30 for larger pictures of the movements.

TEACHING YOUR CHILD TO READ AND WRITE METHOD

With early readers it is best to keep things simple, step by step, and where possible play-based; for that reason, I offer play-based phonics and pre-primer Sight Words as a first step to reading for pre-school or non-reading children of any age.

The first step in teaching your child to read is to teach the 26 phonetic lowercase sounds of the English language.

There are 26 letters in the English alphabet, with a lowercase phonetic sound, "**a**"pple; - "**b**"all; - "**c**"at; - "**d**"og; - "**e**"lephant; - "**f**"lag; - "**g**"ate; - "**h**"orse; - "**i**"gloo; - "**j**"ar; - "**k**"ite; - "**l**"og; - "**m**"at; "**n**"ut; - "**o**"range; - "**p**"in; - "**q**"ueen; - "**r**"est; - "**s**"un; - "**t**"in; - "**u**"p; "**v**"an; - "**w**"et; - fo"**x**"; - "**y**"ellow; - "**z**"ebra.

Generally, the name or capital of letters (such as the "A" in acorn) is not taught until a child has a firm grasp of the basic lowercase alphabet letter sounds.

THE READING METHOD

Show your child the lowercase letter sound "a", while pointing to the "a" say "a" as in "a"pple (do not say the word apple); pointing to the "a" ask your child, "What sound is this?" The child should repeat the sound "a". Use the above method for all the letter sounds of the alphabet.

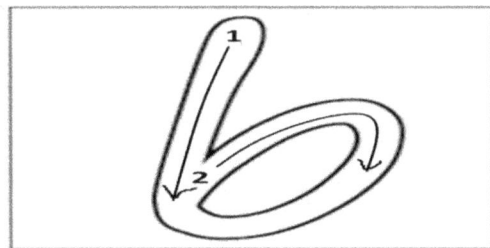

THE WRITING METHOD

Show your child the lowercase letter and say its lowercase sound "a"; point to the letter and ask your child, "What sound is this?" Your child should say the lowercase sound of the letter "a". Trace the letter with your finger by following the numbered lines and say its lowercase letter sound; have your child trace the letter and say its lowercase sound.
Use the above method for all the letter sounds of the alphabet.

TEACHING YOUR CHILD TO READ AND WRITE METHOD

To write the letter start at number 1 and trace the arrowed line; keep your finger or pencil on the letter and go from one number to the next in the number order and trace the line; trace the letter lines as one movement.

NOTE: Some print letters may be formed and taught differently in grade school, or other systems.

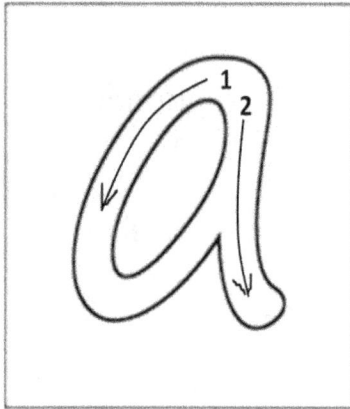

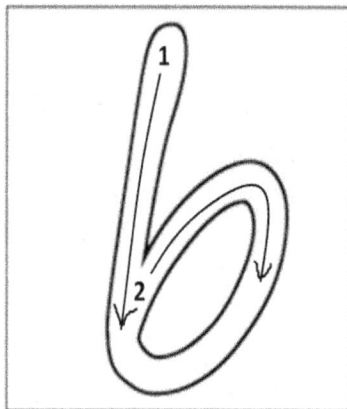

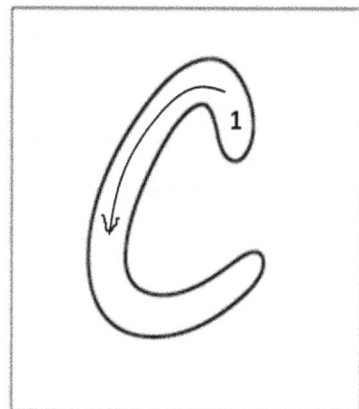

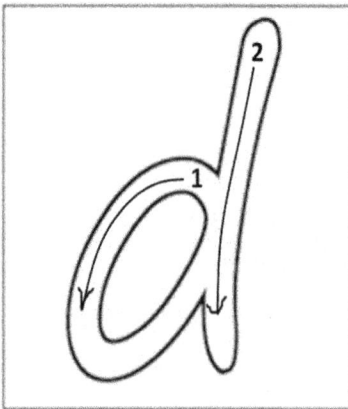

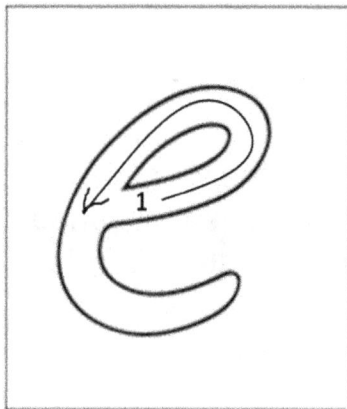

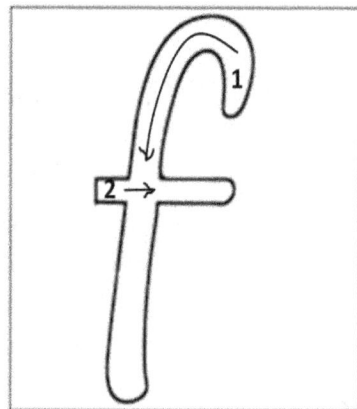

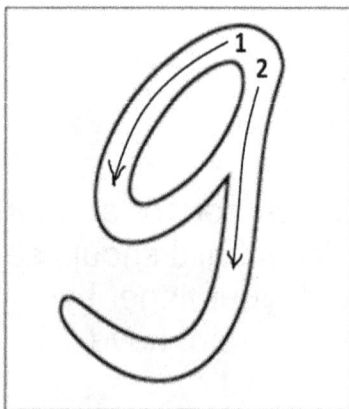

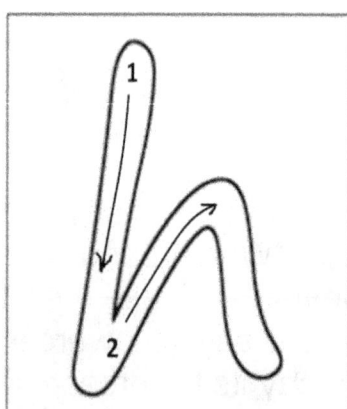

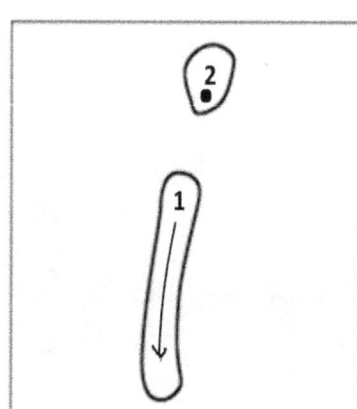

TEACHING YOUR CHILD TO READ AND WRITE METHOD

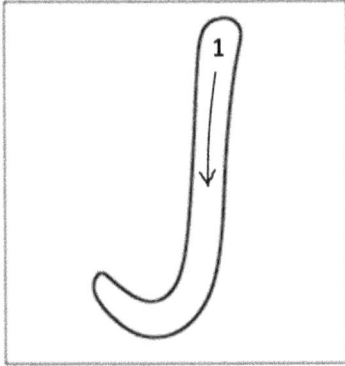

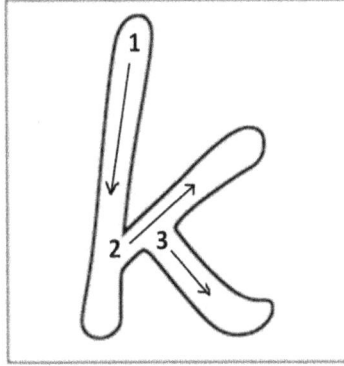

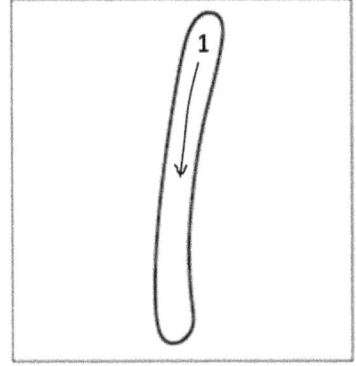

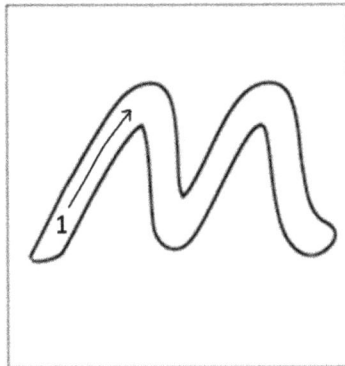

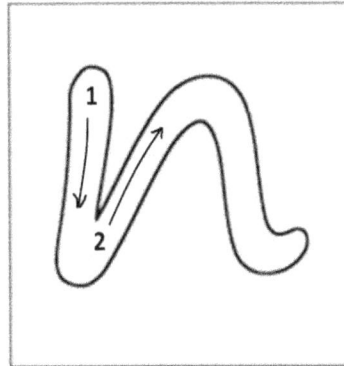

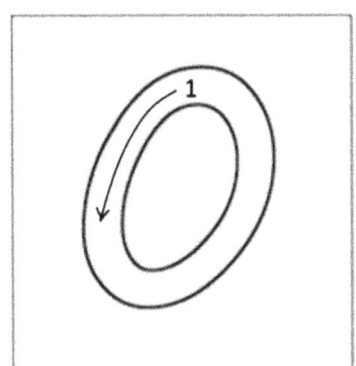

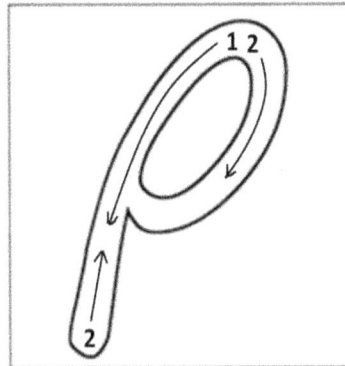

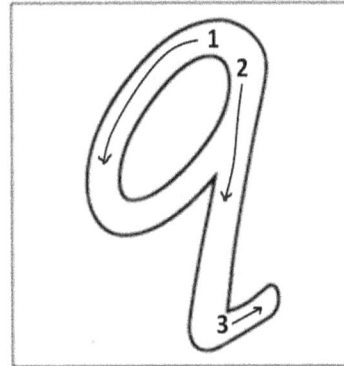

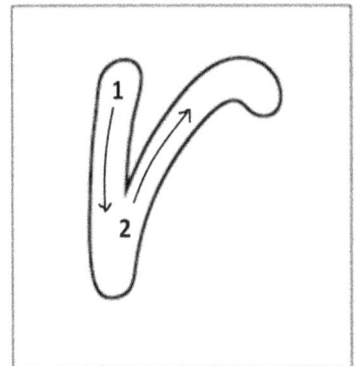

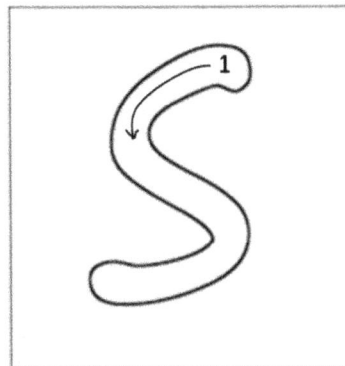

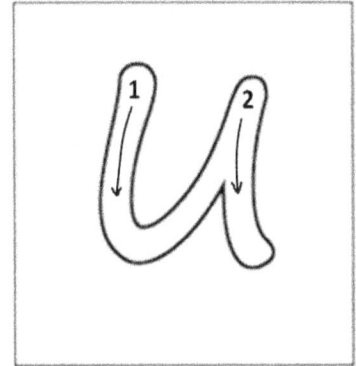

TEACHING YOUR CHILD TO READ AND WRITE METHOD

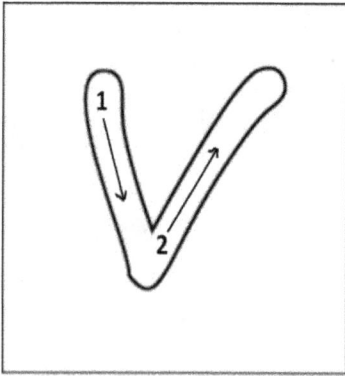

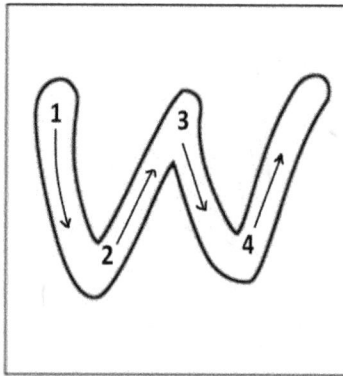

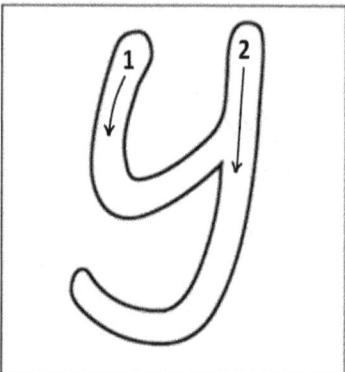

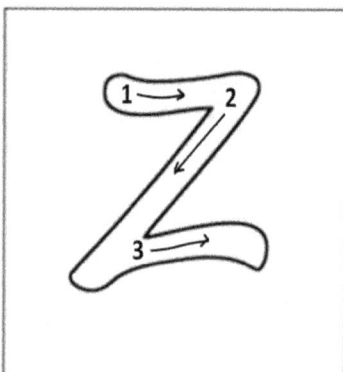

Notes: A pre or grade school child does not have to know the alphabet to do most of the activities presented in this book.

Knowing the numbers 1 to 4 will help children follow the numbered lines.

THE SIDEWAYS 8

This movement is done to help with hand eye coordination, as well as getting the eyes to focus on the left and right of the center line of the body or a page when reading.

This movement is always done before starting the Alphabet Writing activities to help ready the eyes, arm and body coordination needed to complete the movements.

SIDEWAYS 8

How it is done: Show your child how to do the activity.
Have your child Close their left hand with their thumb sticking up,
now hold out the thumb at arm's length; focus eyes on the thumb
and draw an 8 on its side 3 times, up and to the left the width of
the shoulders; do the same with the right hand.

LEFT SIDEWAYS ALPHABET WRITING

How it is done: Trace the letters so your child will see how to do the activity. Have your child start tracing the letter "a" with their left hand pointer finger; then the letters "c", "d", "g", "j", "o" and "q"; do this 3 times; do the same activity with the right hand.

Notes:
Alphabet writing is an activity to help children with:
- Crossing the center line of a page or book.
- Using both eyes to look left and right when reading text in books.
- Recognizing the English alphabet letters in printed form.
- Hand eye coordination required in printing or cursive writing.
- Forming, printing and cursive writing of alphabet letters.

On the following pages are a list of printed and cursive alphabet letters; and drawings of those alphabet letters combined.

The goal is to get your child to use both eyes and cross the midline of the page of text in a fluid movement when reading and writing; you are not teaching the alphabet letters, but you can say the lowercase sound of the letter to prompt the child to trace it.

Notes: Alphabet Writing does not contain the whole alphabet, just the letters that can easily be formed as a continuous motion when writing. All letters follow the arrow to the left, then up or down, depending on the letter; the exception is the "j" which starts in the center and then down; return to the center for each new letter sound.

This activity can be done in the air using the pointer finger, similar to the Sideways 8; on paper; or a blackboard; with eyes closed; left hand then right hand; or on the balance board for increased levels of difficulty.

Notes: Children with vision or learning difficulties may have trouble with this activity; if that is the case, then just do one or two letters at a time; and if the child will allow it, use hand over hand and trace the letters for the child.

When teaching children in home or educational settings, pictures from this book can be copied to be posted on walls or traced as part of an educational activity; otherwise, all copyright restrictions apply.

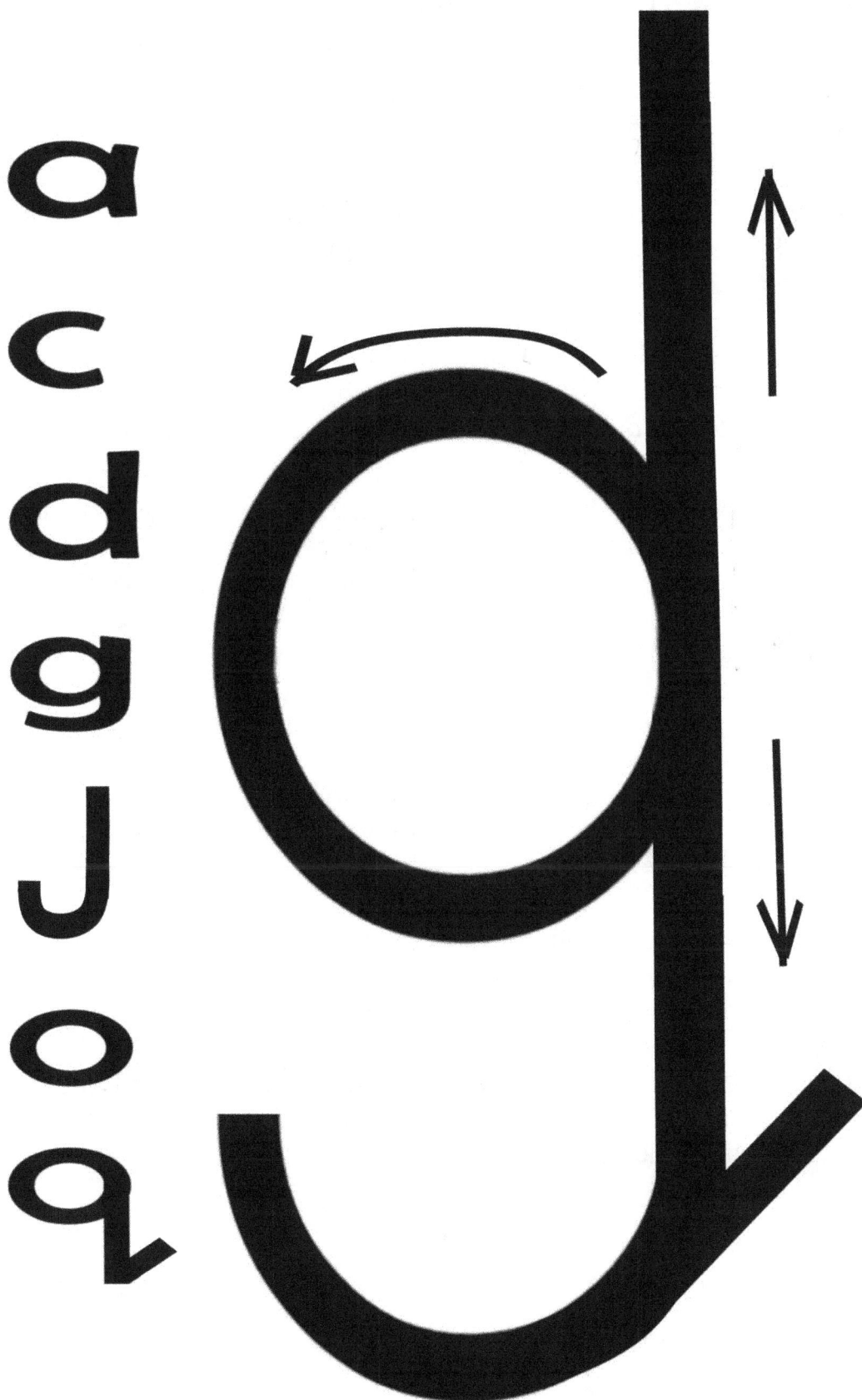

RIGHT SIDEWAYS ALPHABET WRITING

How it is done: Trace the letters so your child will see how to do the activity. Have your child start tracing the letter "b" with their left hand pointer finger; then the letters "h", "l", "m", "n", "p" and "r", do this 3 times with both left and right hands.

Notes: All letters follow the arrows down and to the right; the exception is the "m", which starts up and to the right; return to the center for each new letter sound.

This activity can be done in the air using the pointer finger, similar to the Sideways 8; on paper; or a blackboard; with eyes closed; left hand then right hand; or on the balance board for increased levels of difficulty.

Notes: Children with vision or learning difficulties may have trouble with this activity; if that is the case, then just do one or two letters at a time; and if the child will allow it, use hand over hand and trace the letters for the child.

When teaching children in home or educational settings, pictures from this book can be copied to be posted on walls or traced as part of an educational activity; otherwise, all copyright restrictions apply.

Depending on your hand, eye or brain dominance (which hand, eye or side of your brain you use), you may have to practice the activities before presenting them to your child.

Remember: Sideways Alphabet is about getting your child to use both left and right hands for full brain activation when reading; crossing the midline of the body when reading or writing; and using a continuous flowing motion needed for cursive writing.
Sideways Alphabet is not about teaching the alphabet or alphabet phonic letter sounds; but you can use the lower case phonetic letter sound of the letters to ask the child to trace the letters.

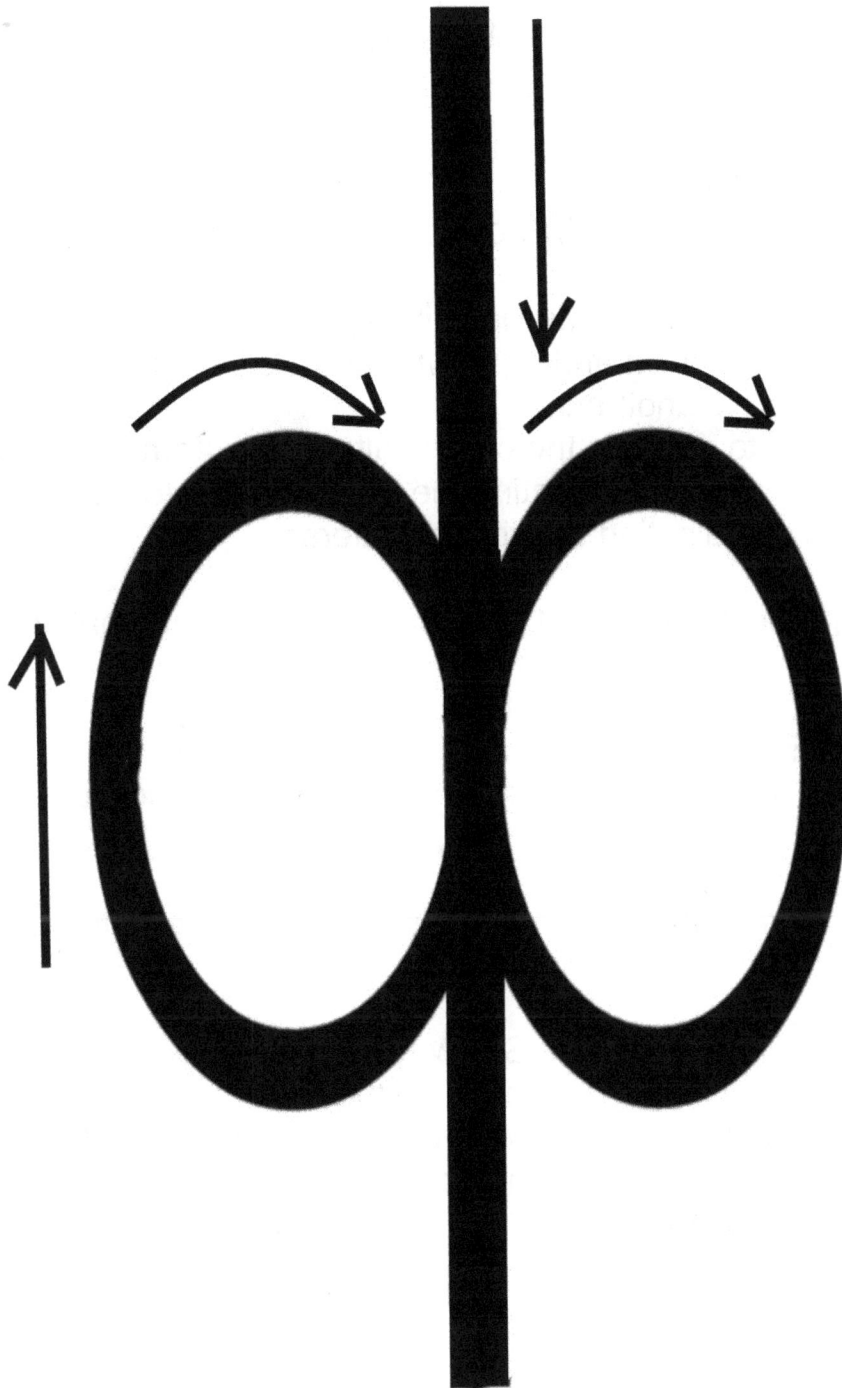

b
h
l
m
n
p
r

LEFT AND RIGHT ALPHABET WRITING

How it is done: Trace the letters so your child will see how to do the activity. Have your child start tracing the letter "a" with their left hand pointer finger; then follow the arrow and trace the next letter "b", then follow the arrows and trace the letters "c", "h", "d", "l", "g", "m", "j", "n", "o", "p", "q" and "r"; do this 3 times with both left and right hands.

Note: After each letter, return to the center to start the next letter.

Notes: By now your child should be familiar with the alphabet letters to the left and right; now we combine left and right; what we are looking for is a steady flow from one letter to another.
With this activity it is best to go slow; the child is alternating from left to right letters, which requires focus and alternating the eyes from left to right; as well as using hand eye coordination to write the letters.

If your child is having difficulty, then just do two, three or four alternating letters at a time.

SETTING A BASELINE
You can use Sideways Alphabet Writing to set a baseline to check for any improvements.

Show your child how to trace the letters and say the lowercase sound of each letter as you trace it.

Have your child trace the Left and Right Sideways Alphabet Writing pages two or three times; time how long they took to do the activity and make note of any errors in tracing the letters; this is your baseline for checking for any improvements; it is expected that over time your child will get quicker and use more fluid smoother movements.

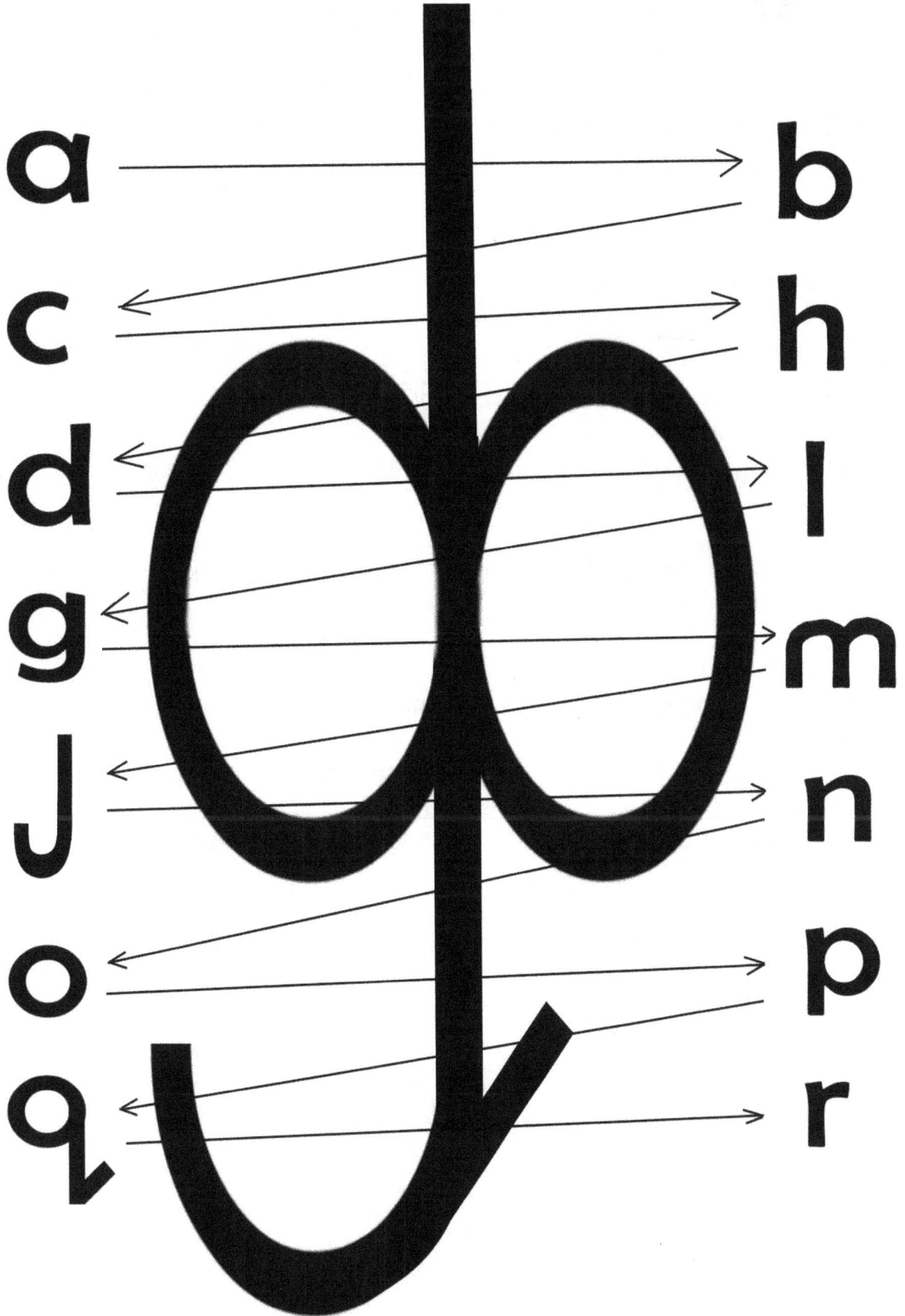

a → b
c ← h
d ← l
g ← m
J ← n
o ← p
q ← r

CURSIVE ALPHABET WRITING

How it is done: Trace all the cursive letters so your child will see how to do the activity. Have your child follow the directional arrows and start tracing the letter "a" with their left hand pointer finger; then trace the next letters "b", "c", "d", "e" and "f"; use the same method to trace the rest of the letters on each line with both hands.

While looking at the page of cursive text, this activity can be done in the air using the pointer finger, similar to the Sideways 8; on paper; or a blackboard; with eyes closed; left hand then right hand; or on the balance board for increased levels of difficulty.

Notes: In English text writing we usually use printing or Cursive handwriting.

There are many opinions how writing should be taught and what English text should be used.

For the purpose of these activities I have used mainly D' Nealian text with some minor changes to make the text more of a continuous flowing text.

The purpose of this activity is to get your child to use both eyes, have hand eye coordination; cross the midline of a page; and write in a continuous flowing movement; essential skills when learning to read and write.

abcdef

ghijkl

mnopqr

stuvwxyz

GRADE SCHOOL LEARNING TO READ SECTION

This section presents some of the same movements and activities that are in the Preschool Section storybooks "A Walk In The Jungle" and "Gordy Visits The Mountains", but in a more adult or grade school way.

WHY LEARN TO READ AND WRITE?

We learn to read and write to share ideas and information; it's as simple as that.

This book is written using Arial text, so for the purposes of you reading and myself conveying my ideas, we are on the same page; you want to learn something, and I want to share something; the medium we are using is reading and writing of Arial text.

WHY USE D' NEALIAN TEXT?

The system was designed as a method to alleviate the problems with teaching children the standard Zaner-Bloser script method and the subsequent difficulty transitioning to cursive writing. D'Nealian manuscript form has many similarities to the cursive version. In theory, it is easier for children to learn and acquire basic handwriting skills using this method than traditional cursive writing (courtesy of Wikipedia.org).

D'Nealian Manuscript	Arial Text	D'Nealian Cursive
Aa Bb Cc Dd Ee Ff Gg Hh	Aa Bb Cc Dd Ee Ff Gg Hh	a b c d e f g h i j k
Ii Jj Kk Ll Mm Nn Oo Pp	Ii Jj Kk Ll Mm Nn Oo Pp	l m n o p q r s t
Qq Rr Ss Tt Uu Vv Ww Xx	Qq Rr Ss Tt Uu Vv Ww Xx	u v w x y z
Yy Zz 0 1 2 3 4 5 6 7 8 9	Yy Zz 1 2 3 4 5 6 7 8 9	A B C D E F G H I
		J K L M N O P Q R
		S T U V W X Y Z
		1 2 3 4 5 6 7 8 9 10

MOVE AND IMPROVE DEVELOPMENTAL MOVEMENTS

Over the years I have found many methods that have helped me reduce stress and improve my thinking and communication skills; those methods have been adapted and together form the "Move and Improve" movements.

I have used the movements with preschool children, special needs children, grade school children, adults and myself personally for 25 years.
Through observation there have been various benefits for myself and those whom I have taught; my claims are based on those observations.

I suggest doing the following movements before starting any activities:
Listening Ears; Water; Energy Boost; Crossovers and Connections
(All movements are in order as they appear in "A Walk In The
Jungle" storybook.)

SOME POSSIBILITIES

☺ Increased self-esteem.
☺ Increased self-control.
☺ Calms and relaxes children and adults.
☺ Creates a calm and relaxed environment.
☺ Overcome learning stress.
☺ Make changes in routine easier.
☺ Helps children be more self directing.
☺ Empower parents and teachers to make a difference in their children's growth.

My general feeling is that doing the movements will at least give some enjoyment; and a sense of wellbeing.

These movements are from the storybook "A Walk In The Jungle" activities", which were designed to give children and adults meaningful day activities; and developmental movements to enhance learning abilities.

The activities in this section are presented in adult form, so you can present them to children in the correct way.

This section explains how to do each movement and gives a visual, printable page picture, to help guide you when presenting the activity to others; You can also view the storybook movements on my website at: https://howtoteachchildrentoread.ca

Each activity is placed on its own individual page, please feel free to copy and post the pages as part of your lesson plan; all other copyright restrictions apply.

Consistency is the key when presenting the movements to others; as the teacher, you always present the correct movement.
Children will try to copy the movement but may not have enough fine motor skills to do the exact movement.
If a child is doing the movement incorrectly, just say, "Watch me", instead of correcting them.

FRIENDLY WAVE

May help with: Listening, balance and memory.

Why it is important: Developing the ability to listen, retain information and have whole body co-ordination are essential skills for easy learning and good social interaction.

How it is done: Tilt your head, placing your ear on your shoulder, while extending your arm forward; with your hand draw an infinity sign (an 8 on its side) the width of your shoulders, focusing your eyes beyond the fingertips; your body and arm move as one unit with no twisting at the hips.
Do several times with both arms.

LISTENING EARS

May help with: Listening and focusing skills.

Why it is important: Attention is taken away from other activities while getting participants to focus and listen.

How it is done: Grasp each ear with the thumb on the inside rim and the pointer finger on the outside rim; uncurl the ear down to the ear lobe using the pointer finger along with the thumb; bring pointer finger and thumb back to the top of the ear and repeat several times.

This activity can be used to see if children are paying attention; and when transitioning children to new activities.

WATER

May help with: Learning and energy levels.

Why it is important: Water helps conduct the electrical and chemical processes of the brain for clear thinking.

How it is done: Having a water bottle close by is an easy way to take a drink during the activity.

ENERGY BOOST

May help with: Increased energy and relaxation.

Why it is important: Being relaxed and energetic makes learning easier.

How it is done: Place your hand on your neck (palm on the Adam's apple) with thumb on one side and fingers on the other; move your hand down until you feel your collar-bone, jump over the collar-bone and massage the soft spots between the next set of ribs and the collar-bone; place your other hand on your belly button (do not massage with this hand); switch both hands and repeat for about 30 seconds.

This activity can be used when you are feeling tired and need a quick energy boost

CROSSOVERS

May help with: Accessing the whole brain, crossing the midline for reading, comprehension and body coordination.

Why it is important: Using the left and right side of the body at the same time accesses both sides of the brain at the same time.

How it is done: Lift your left leg and touch your left knee with your right hand; put the foot down and lift your right leg and touch your right knee with your left hand; repeat, three or more times.
Participants having difficulty can match colored bands or stickers placed on opposite hands and knees.

CONNECTIONS

May help with: De-stressing and easier learning.

Why it is important: Being relaxed and focused helps make learning easier and improves self-esteem.

How it is done: Ask the participants to stand, or lie on the floor, cross their feet at the ankles and give themselves a big hug by placing their hands under each arm pit; can be done standing, sitting or lying down.

BACK ARCH

May help with: Improved posture, concentration and tension release.

Why it is important: After sitting for long periods, slightly arching the back helps release body tension, improve posture and concentration.

How it is done: Resting on your elbows, lie face down on the floor and slightly arch your back by lifting your head backwards; relax by bringing your head down; repeat several times.

MASSAGE YAWN

May help with: Energy and verbal expression.

Why it is important: Having more energy, a relaxed jaw and facial muscles make it easier for participants to think clearly, communicate, speak or sing. The roaring sound helps participants express themselves.

How it is done: Put your fingers on your cheeks; find the pivotal points of the jaw by opening and closing the jaw; while yawning, massage the pivot points with the fingers; make a yawning or roaring sound.

TENSION AND RELEASE

May help with: Relaxation and body control.

Why it is important: The movement teaches how to use tension and release to gain body control and relax.

How it is done: Reach straight up as high as you can; spread your fingers wide and push your feet down to the ground; push and reach together, this puts the body into tension; sway from one foot to the other, which can release tension; repeat several times.

VISUALIZATION

May help with: Visualization and problem solving.

Why it is important: Being able to picture what is going on in the mind's eye is an important skill in problem solving.

How it is done: Close your eyes and imagine the sun as various colors, shapes and sizes; or imagine objects children are familiar with.

THE BALANCE BOARD

An exceptional piece of equipment that may help
children and adults develop their full potential.

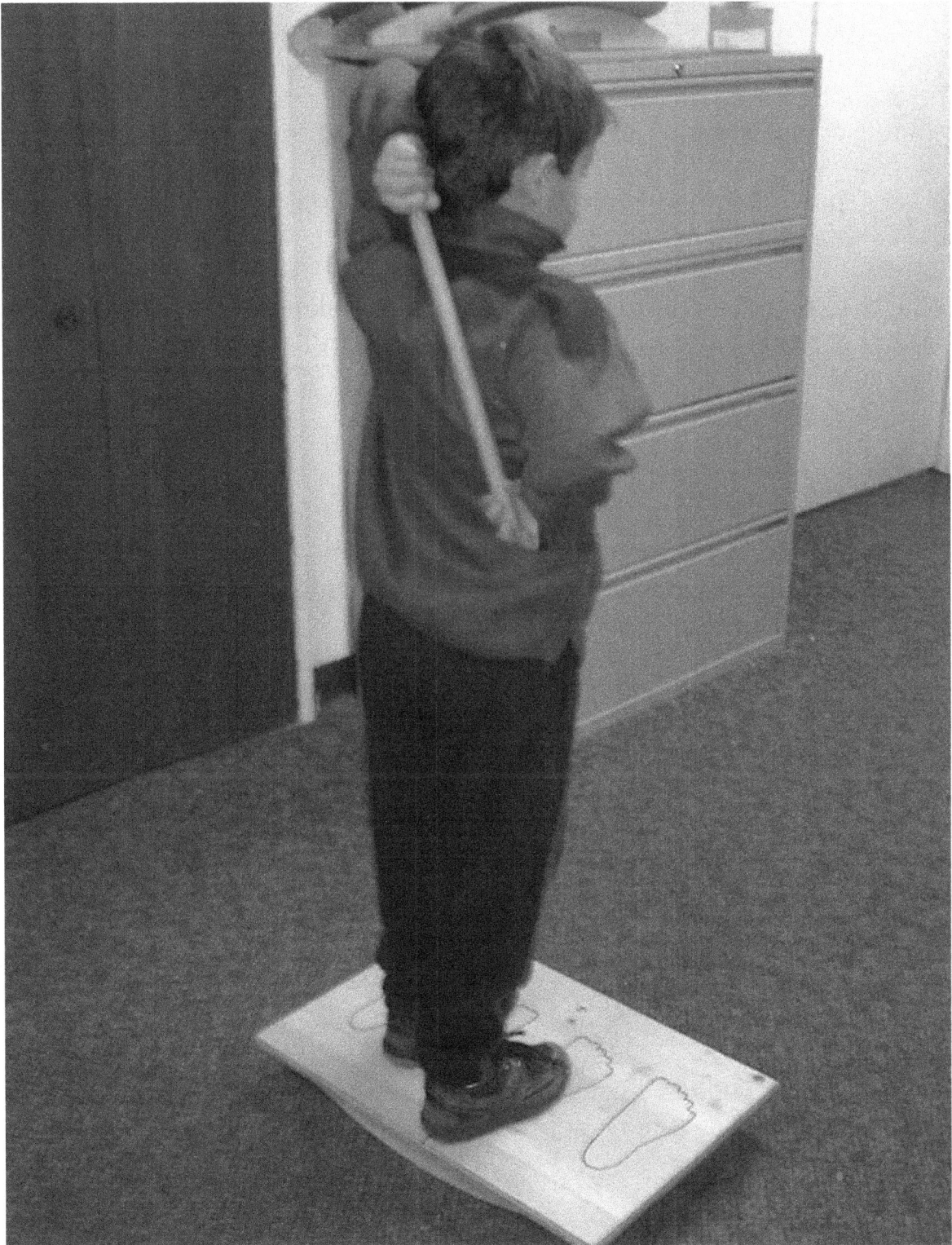

THE BALANCE BOARD

The purpose of the Balance Board is to switch on the body's vestibular balance system while doing a task or activity.

In the book "The Throwing Madonna" Dr. William Calvin puts forward the theory that throwing spears at a target and running on large rocks led humans to develop bigger brains.

The Balance Board activities use balance, throwing at targets, and sequencing activities to help with whole Brain and body integration.

The adjustable Balance Board is adjusted to its tipping point between being able to balance and not being able to balance.

Some care must be exercised when using the Balance Board, especially if the user is prone to seizures, has poor balance or body coordination.

Some concerns are:
- Spinning can cause seizures, especially for those that may have sensory difficulties.
- Getting on and off the Balance Board can be difficult for some people, usually due to the sudden movement of the board.
- Always consult a doctor, or sensory therapist If you observe sensory difficulties such as: seeks or avoids sensory stimulation; poor coordination; unsure of body position in space; easily distracted; not able to focus; unusual behavior; and running hand along walls.

I have used Balance Board activities with:
- Babies, by holding them in a sitting position on the board.
- Pre-school children, as part of my storybook activity.
- With school children and college students studying for tests.
- Special needs adults and the elderly; they all seemed to enjoy the activities.

Notes: I have personally used the board to help center and focus myself before the day starts; and to help with my balance in Martial Arts.

When used in an educational setting, the activities can be printed and placed on the wall as a reminder of what to do.

I cannot guarantee results by practicing these activities; the benefits listed are purely based on observed benefits to myself and others in my care.
I suggest you try them; it is my hope that they work for you, as they did for me.

THINGS WE CAN DO ON THE BALANCE BOARD

The Rotational Balance Board

This Balance Board Is generally used to help develop spatial awareness (where you and objects are in space) and help with vestibular difficulties (The vestibular system controls movement and balance.)

SAFETY: The Balance Board should always be set-up on a non-slip surface such as a carpet.

we can lie and spin

we can sit or kneel

we can stand and spin

ADJUSTABLE BALANCE BOARD ACTIVITIES

Pass the Koosh Ball

Study for a test

Pass the stick

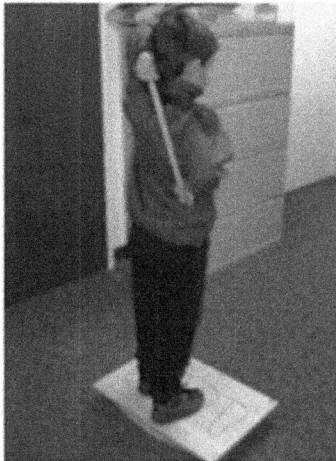

Eyes closed

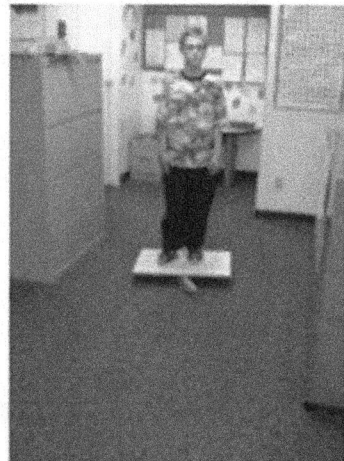

Read a book

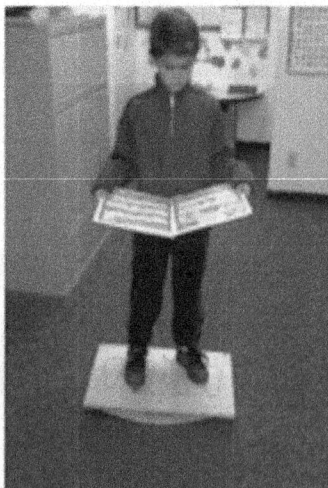

Pass ball to partner

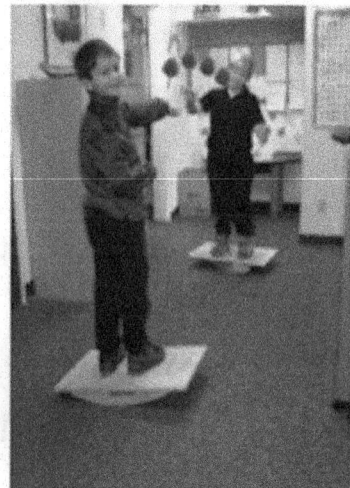

PASS THE STICK OVER YOUR SHOULDER

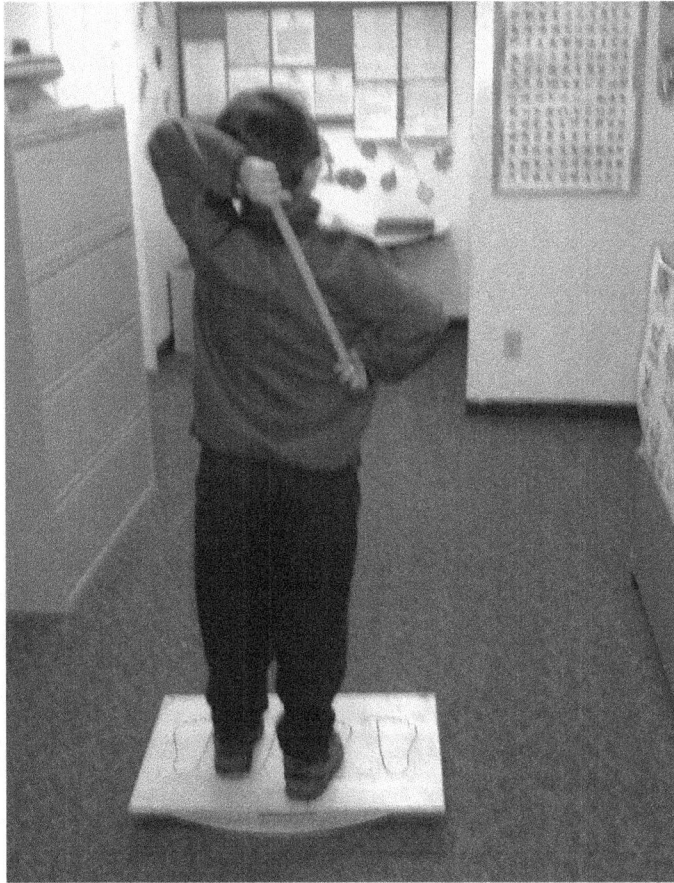

How it is done: Adjust Balance Board level of difficulty; with your left hand pass the stick over your left shoulder and grab it with your right hand behind your back; then, with your right hand pass the stick over your right shoulder and grab it with your left hand.

Count out loud the number of passes in 1 minute; count to 100 (or another number) in 2s, 3s, or 5s, then back from 100 in 2s, 3s, or 5s.

Possible benefits:
> More able to figure out difficult tasks.
> Increased coordination and concentration.
> More able to sequence numbers.
> Increase in memory.

Note: Counting will depend on a child's ability and level of development; either make it easier or harder, so a child will be successful.

AWARENESS OF WHERE THINGS ARE IN SPACE.
THROW KOOSH BALL AT A TARGET

How it is done: Adjust Balance Board level of difficulty; Stand on the Balance Board and throw a bean bag or koosh ball at the target; throw two koosh balls at the target, one with the left hand, then one with the right hand.

Possible benefits:

>Increased hand - eye coordination.
>Awareness of timing and sequencing abilities.
>Awareness of where things are in space.

PASS THE KOOSH BALL FROM ONE HAND TO THE OTHER

How it is done: Adjust the Balance Board level of difficulty; bounce koosh ball in palms of hands; count to 100 (or another number) in 2s, 3s, or 5s, then back from 100 in 2s, 3s, or 5s.

Possible benefits:
>Increased hand/eye coordination.
>Being able to do work without thinking.
>Sequencing information.
>Counting skills.

Note: Counting will depend on a child's ability and level of development; either make it easier or harder, so a child will be successful.

READ A BOOK OR STUDY

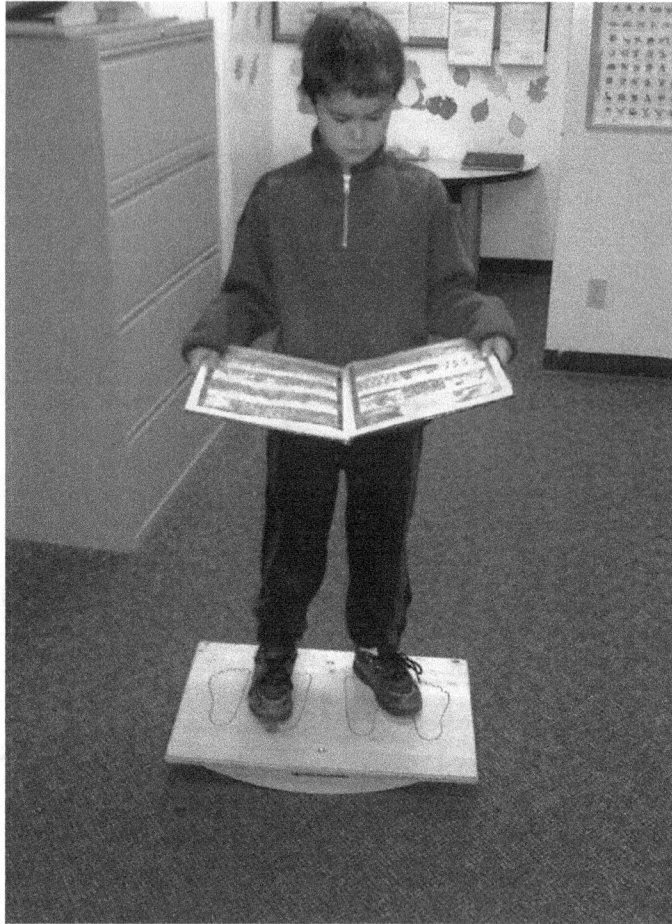

How it is done: Adjust Balance Board level of difficulty; read aloud for 1 minute; hum a song for 1 minute; repeat reading then humming.

Possible benefits:

> Switching from left to right brain.
> Improved reading skills.
> Improved thinking skills.

Note: Balancing, reading and humming activate more parts of the Brain at the same time, for a more whole Brain integration activity.

PASS THE KOOSH BALL TO A PARTNER

How it is done: Adjust Balance Board level of difficulty; pass the koosh ball to your partner with your left hand and catch with the right hand; pass the koosh ball with your right hand and catch with the left hand; pass 2 koosh balls, throw and catch one left and one right.

Possible benefits:

Ability to process sensory information.
Increased choice making and attention.
Improved eye tracking.
Improved organization and social skills.
Crossing the midline of the body.

KEEP YOUR EYES CLOSED

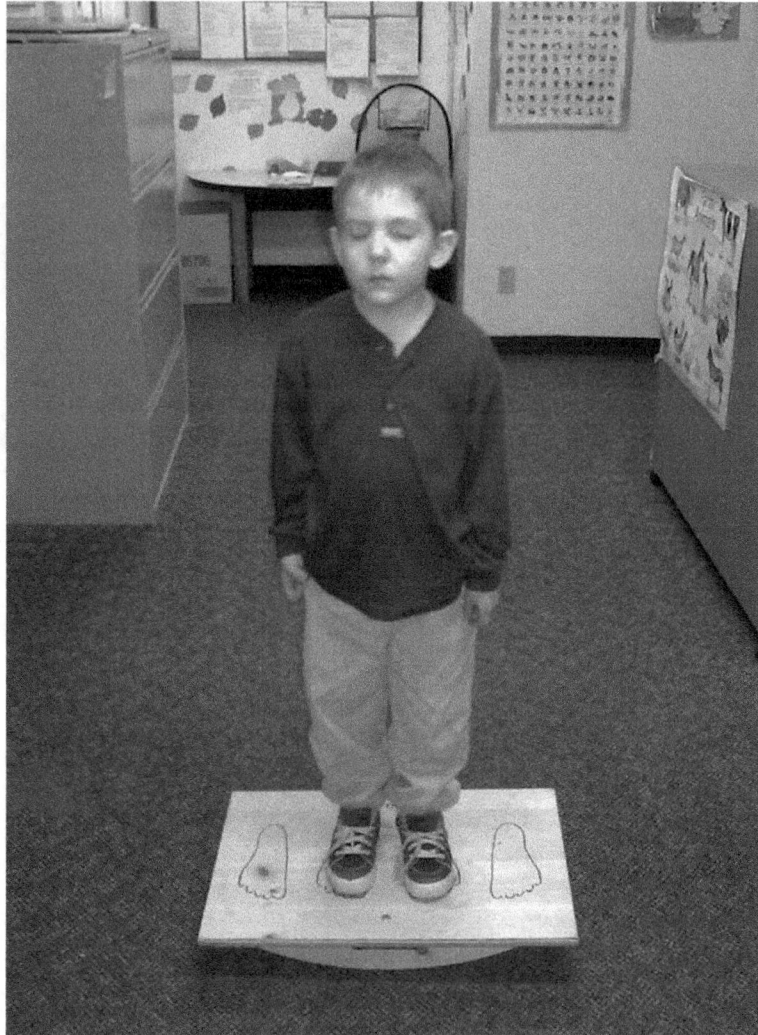

How it is done: Adjust Balance Board level of difficulty; stand on the board with eyes closed and arms down (If you feel like you are falling over, then open your eyes.)

Possible benefits:

    Increased concentration.
    Improved balance.
    Awareness of where you are in space.

STUDY SPELLING TESTS

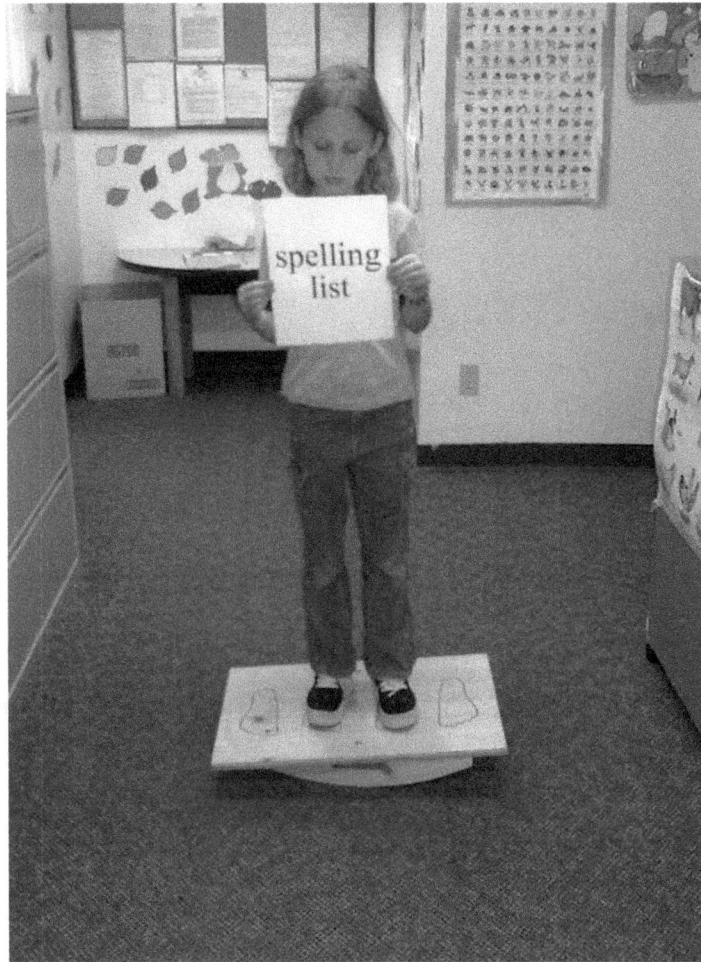

How it is done: Adjust Balance Board level of difficulty; stand on board and read spelling list quietly; say the word, and then spell it out; read the word, close your eyes and see the word; then spell the word out loud; have a partner spell each word and you repeat the word.

Possible benefits:
>
> Increased memory.
> Retaining what is read.
> Visualization.

THE ADJUSTABLE BALANCE BOARD

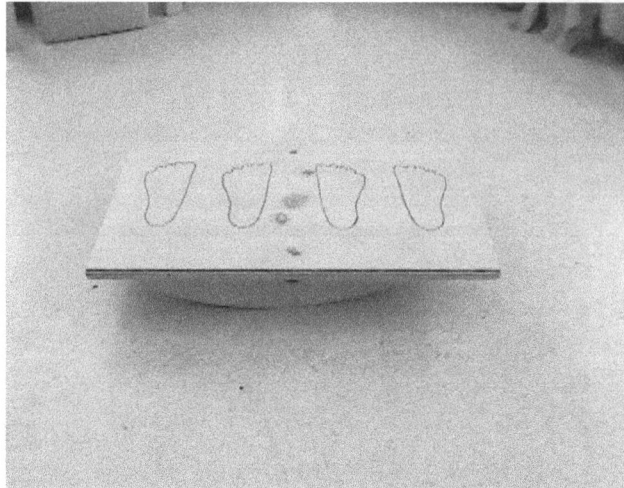

The Balance Board should be placed on a non-slip surface.

This board can be used to activate the vestibular system; which may help with easier learning of information; focusing the mind; balancing the body; and mind body integration.

This Balance Board can be adjusted to easy or difficult by rotating the semi-circular rockers under the board.

The adjustable Balance Board is adjusted to its tipping point between being able to balance and not being able to balance.

Adjust the board as children become more adept and familiar with it.

Notes: I recommend that you always consult a doctor before you attempt any Balance Board exercise.

Always watch for children falling, when they get on or off the board.

Balance Boards can be purchased from:
https://howtoteachchildrentoread.ca/

HOW TO MAKE THE BALANCE BOARD

The Adjustable Balance Board:

The board Is made from ¾ inch good one side plywood.

The boards optimal size is 24 inches x 16 inches (you will get 11 from a 4 foot x 8 foot sheet of plywood).

The board has adjustable rockers, to adjust the level of difficulty.

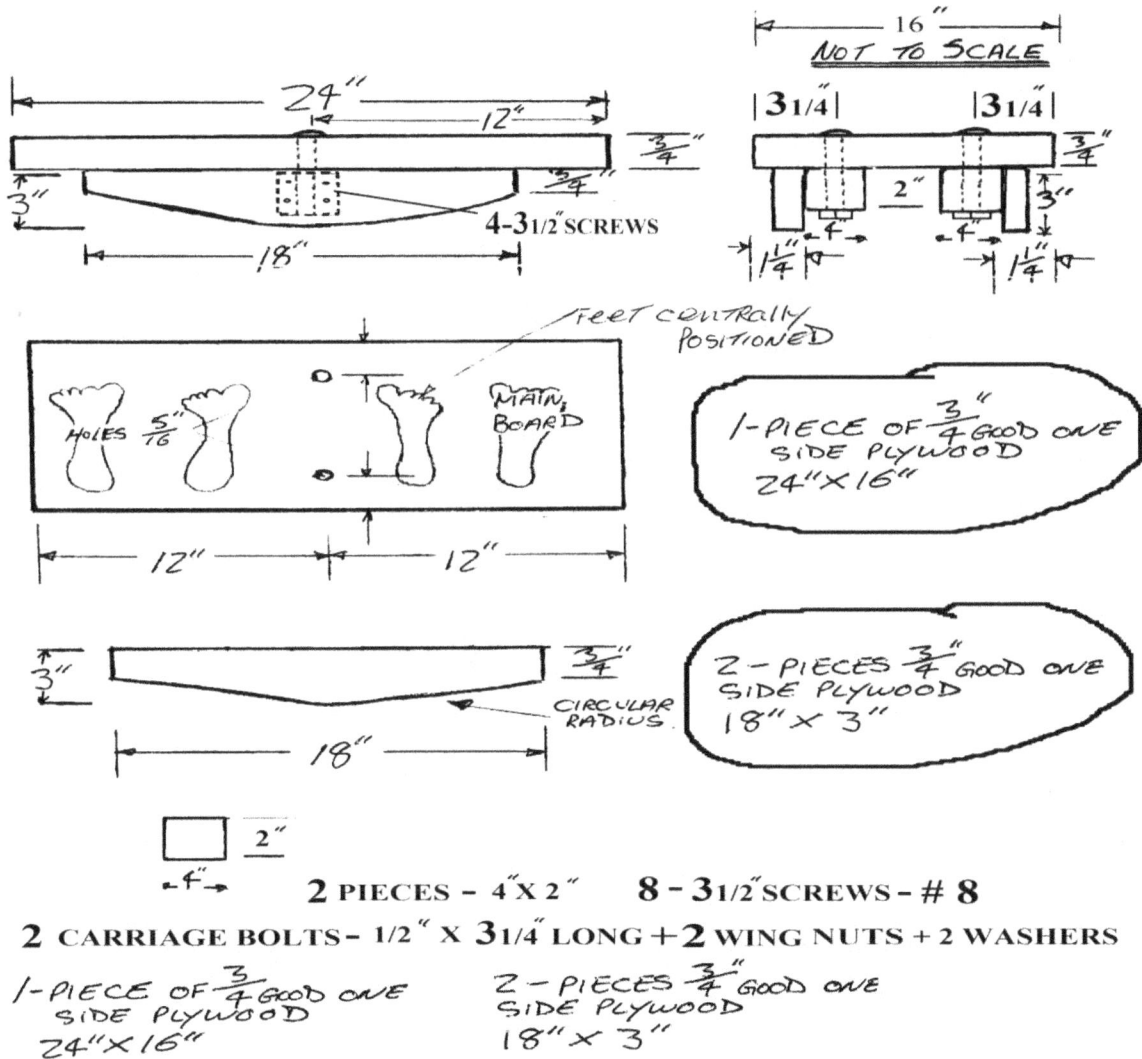

The Passing Stick

Made from a 1/2 inch piece of round wood doweling, 24 inch or 12 inches (if you have more flexibility) and rounded off at both ends.

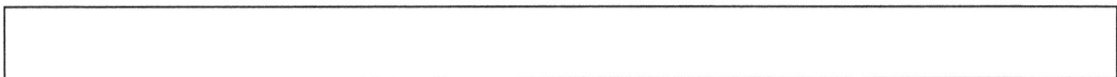

HOW TO MAKE THE ROTATIONAL BALANCE BOARD

The Rotational Balance Board:

- The board Is made from 2 pieces of ¾ inch good one side plywood.
- The boards optimal size is 16 inches in diameter. You will get 9 boards (18 pieces) from a 4 foot x 8 foot sheet of plywood.
- A 12 inch Lazy Susan rotational cupboard bearing is placed centrally between two pieces of plywood.

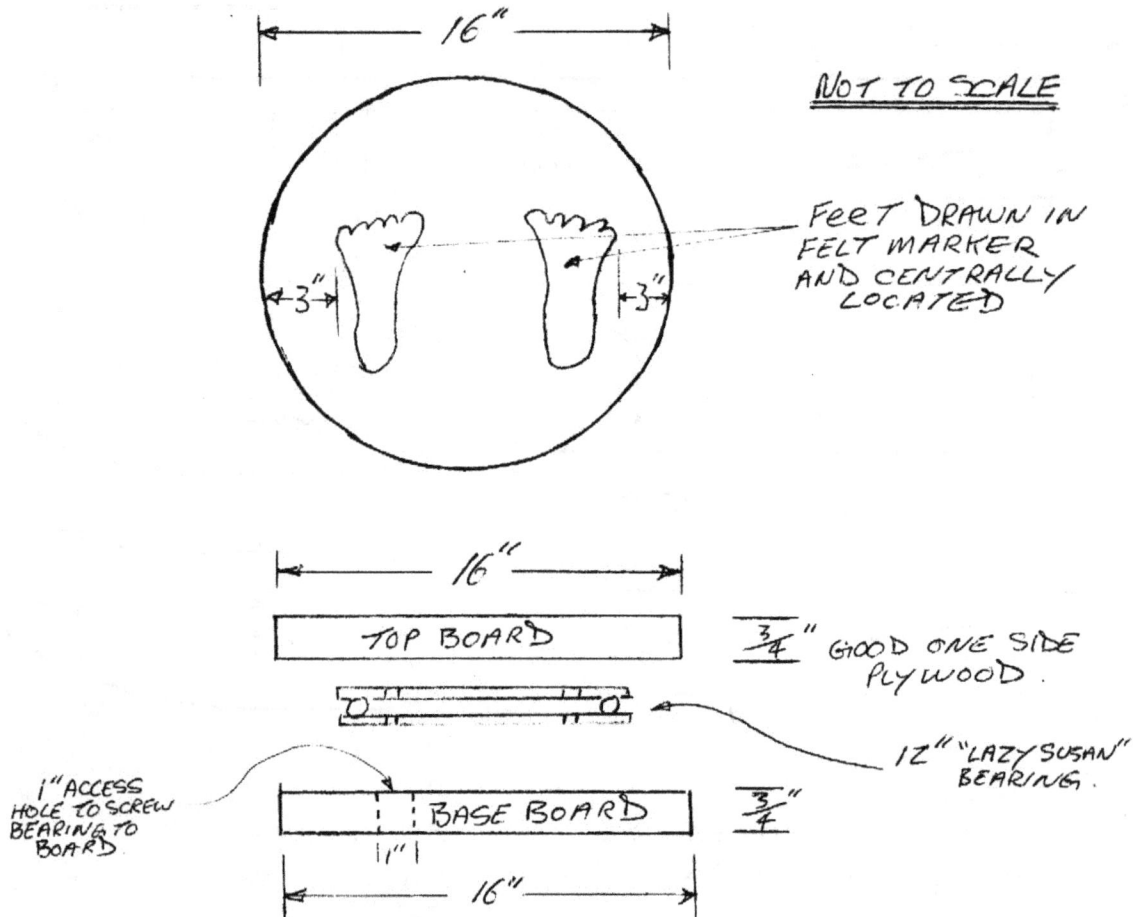

NOT TO SCALE

FeeT DRAWN IN FELT MARKER AND CENTRALLY LOCATED

16"
3"   3"

16"

TOP BOARD   ¾" GOOD ONE SIDE PLYWOOD.

12" "LAZY SUSAN" BEARING.

1" ACCESS HOLE TO SCREW BEARING TO BOARD.

BASE BOARD   ¾"

1"

16"

The board can be clear laquered and have a sprinkling of sand applied, to give a non slip surface to the board.

Materials needed:
2 PIECES OF 16" DIAMETER GOOD ONE SIDE Plywood.
1 "LAZY SUSAN" BEARING
SOME SCREWS FOR THE BEARING MOUNT.

MOVE TO IMPROVE OBSTACLE COURSE

This obstacle course is designed to help children develop the skills needed to read, write and do sequencing activities.

- Set-up the "Move To Improve Obstacle Course" according to the layout sheet shown on the next page.
- Foam pads go under tables, the table can be covered to the floor with a blanket.
- The Balance Board is placed on a carpet or rubberized surface (to reduce the risk of the board slipping).
- The Balance Board activity is shown in the Balance Board section.
- The "Move To Improve Obstacle Course" can be painted on the floor.
- You can use rubberized craft material to make lines, arrows and foot markers; or purchase from https://howtoteachchildrentoread.ca

Always show the children how to do the activity and start with Listening Ears; Water; Energy Boost; Crossovers and Connections

HEEL TO TOE AND BALANCE: Helps with balance, sequencing, awareness of gravity and space.

How it is done: Walk slowly over the line or balance beam (a piece of sanded smooth wood 1"x6"x48") by placing one foot in front of the other (heel to toe); hold the hands of unsteady children if necessary; if the children are confident then walk heel to toe backwards.

Why it is important: Sequential movement helps with basic math, logic and reasoning skills. This movement helps the child develop an awareness of both sides of the body, gravity, space and balance. Use of both brain hemispheres as well as the development of the vestibular system can make learning easier.

JUMP USING BOTH FEET: Helps with use of both sides of the body

How it is done: Both arms and knees swing up together, as you jump and raise both feet off the ground and move forward.

Why it is important: Lifting the whole body vertically off the ground demonstrates children's whole body coordination and an awareness of their relationship to space.

MOVE TO IMPROVE OBSTACLE COURSE

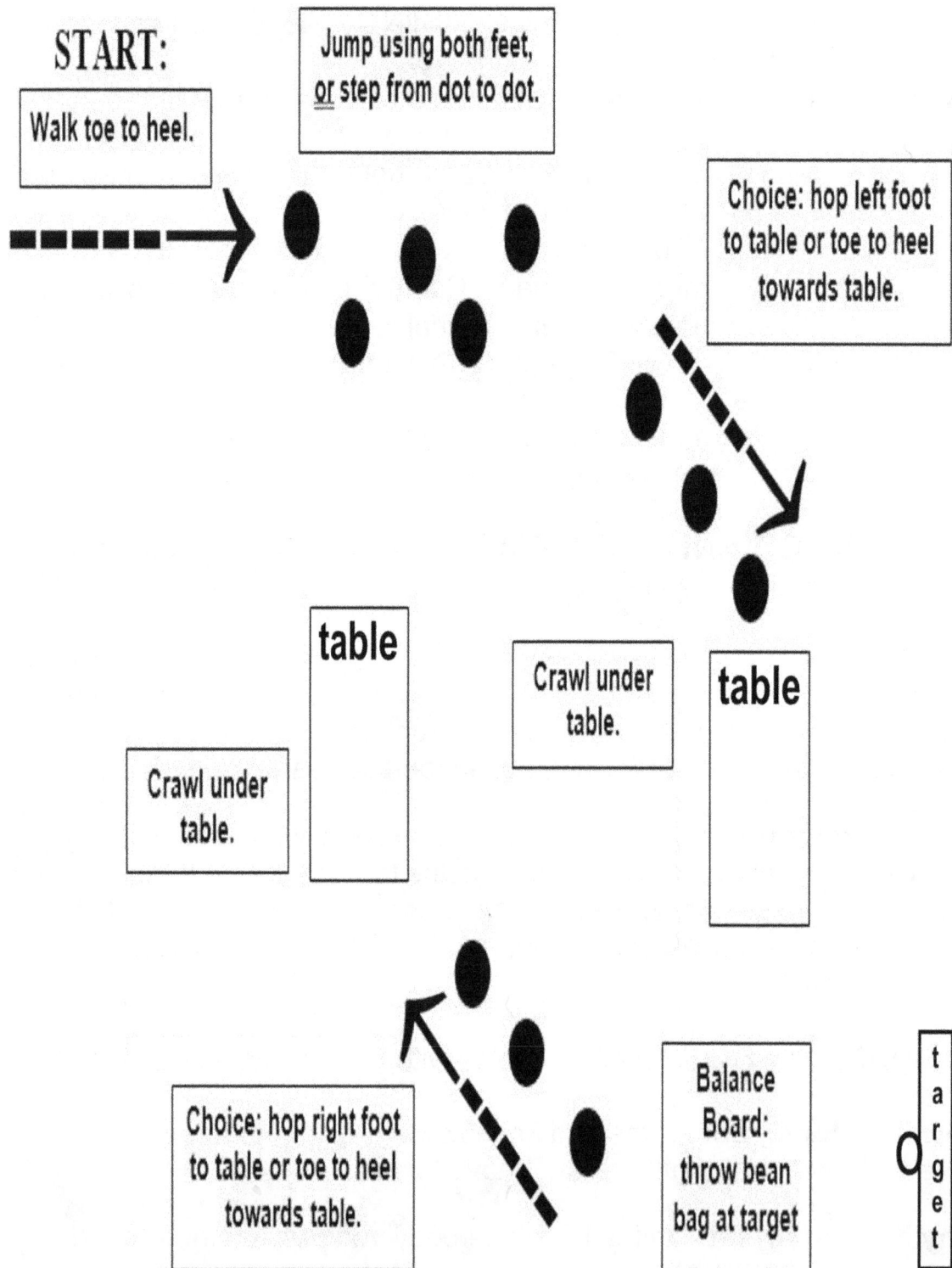

START:

Walk toe to heel.

Jump using both feet, or step from dot to dot.

Choice: hop left foot to table or toe to heel towards table.

Crawl under table.

table

Crawl under table.

table

Choice: hop right foot to table or toe to heel towards table.

Balance Board: throw bean bag at target

target

MOVE TO IMPROVE OBSTACLE COURSE

HOPPING: Helps with postural control of the whole body.

How it is done: Generally, toddlers will not be able to hop on one foot. Older children should be able to hop; you could also try hopscotch games. Have younger children hold onto the back of a chair and hop on one foot.

Why it is important: Hopping helps to gain postural control of the whole body and awareness of the shift in gravity as the child moves.

CRAWLING: Helps with using both sides of the brain together.

How it is done: The children crawl through a tunnel or under a table; entice the children through the tunnel by waiting on the other side of the tunnel and encouraging them to come to you; give lots of praise.

Why it is important: Crawling is a basic developmental stage which has a bilateral movement (the opposite arm and leg work together). This leads to being able to use both sides of the brain together and develops physical skills to help children learn how to read and write.

BALANCE BOARD: Helps with developing the vestibular balance system.

How it is done: Children stand on the Balance Board and throw a bean bag at a target; an adjustable Balance Board can be set to increase the level of difficulty; the target can be anything, preferably a smaller target to increase accuracy in throwing.

Why it is important: Developing the vestibular or balance system is said to help children learn easier and develop the brain.
The book "The Throwing Madonna" by William Calvin puts forward the idea that humans developed bigger brains through hunting and movements such as throwing spears at a target or jumping on rocks.

Shown on the opposite page are pictures of the obstacle course painted on a concrete floor, with rubber mats to crawl on; what to do instructions on sheets of paper; and a Balance Board with a target pinned on a wall.

walk heel to toe

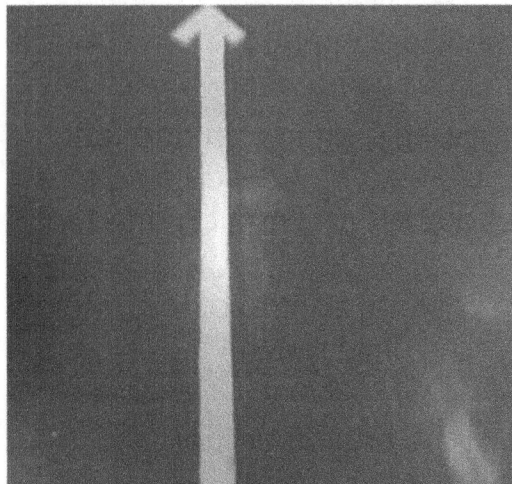

jump with two feet

hop left foot

crawl

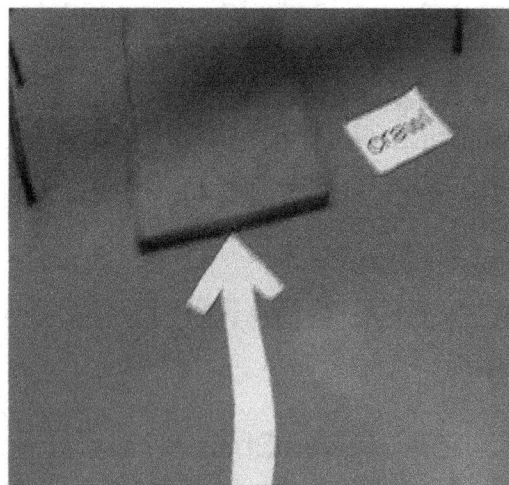

hop right foot

balance on board

OBSTACLE COURSE PRODUCTS

Arrow Markers

Balance Beam

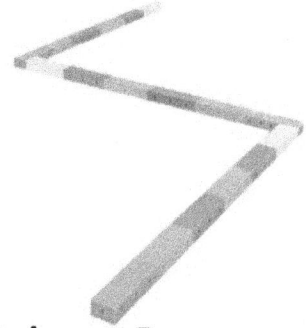

Balance Beam

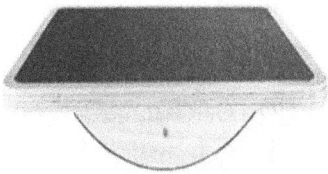

Balance Board

Rotational Board

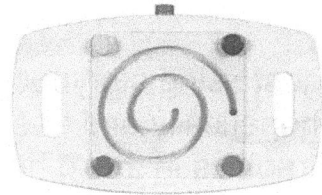

Balance Maze

Balance Pods

Balance Stones

Hand Floor Markers

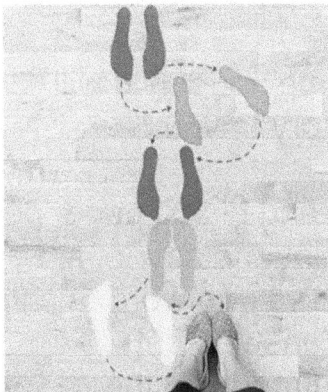

Feet Floor Markers

Shape Obstacles

Crawling Tunnel

https://howtoteachchildrentoread.ca

PRESCHOOL LEARNING TO READ SECTION

There are many opinions, studies and methods about teaching or not teaching preschool children to read; putting all that aside, I suggest teaching preschool children how to read by reading them a story; showing them the printed words in storybooks; and providing a learning to read, play-based environment.

Story telling is one of the first steps to teaching your preschool child how to read. Storytelling is as easy as reading your child three letter word stories and then showing your child the letter sounds and written words in the story.

I suggest using storybooks that have three letter words that can be sounded out phonetically and easily remembered by the beginning reader.
The graphics in these books should be black and white line drawings which will not strain a developing preschool child's eyes.

shown on the opposite page is an example of the type of storybook I suggest you read to a preschool child (example from Play-Based Ways To Teach Your Child To Read).

KEEP IT SIMPLE
Find a comfortable place to sit, so you and your child will be able to see and read the story together.

As you read the story point to each word with your pointer finger.

My suggestion is to read the story a few times; over time your child will remember the story and may even want to read the story to you.

After you have read the story you can stop at the end and pick a page; point to each word and sound out each letter; you would point and say "c, a, t", while saying each letter sound separately but together as one word "c a t"; ask your child, "What word is this?" Your child should answer "cat".
You are teaching the story words as sight words but introducing the phonetic letter sounds of those words; some sight words may not be able to be sounded out.

Note: Preschool children love repetition and may choose one story for you to read over and over; that's OK, just keep reading, pointing out the words and saying the phonetic sounds of the letters, one page per story reading.

sad bob sat

sad bob had a hut

big log hut

bob sat on bed

Storybooks for beginner readers should have: no color; black and white line drawings to help reduce eyestrain in preschool children; 3 letter words that can be sounded out; 3, 4, or 5 word sentences; large letters; and with no punctuation or capitals.

FOR THOSE THAT WANT TO KNOW MORE

Question:
Why do you use black and white drawings in your storybooks?

If you are teaching your child to read using storybooks, then black and white line drawings are easier for preschool children to focus on while showing them the text of the story; black and white line drawings may also reduce eye strain in preschool children.
If you are not teaching your child to read from storybooks, then I would use storybooks with color and use the storybook as a cooperative parent/child activity.

Question:
Should I teach my preschool child to read, isn't it too early?

If you are using play and telling stories to teach a preschool child how to read, then in my opinion, "No, it is not too early." Play and storytelling are natural activities that preschool children enjoy doing; so, why not guide the process towards learning to read; children learn from something they enjoy doing.

Question:
Why are certain movements essential for my child's development?

Science is proving that preschool children's brains develop in the early years by providing certain movements and activities such as crawling, hopping, balance and sequential movements.

The bottom line is this:

non stimulated brain

fewer pathways to enable thought development

stimulated brain

a rich network of pathways to permit complex thinking

FOR THOSE THAT WANT TO KNOW MORE

Question:
What if my child does not want to learn to read?

My answer is, "Do not teach them to read"; instead, set up a good reading environment in your home; offer play based activities and toys that encourage learning to read; take your child to the library and let them choose which books they like; read stories to your child; point out the words and letter sounds in a matter of fact way; over time your child will learn to recognize letter sounds and words that tell the story.
If a child resists or does not want to do a reading type of activity,
"THEN STOP!"

Question:
My 2 year old gets upset and resists everything I ask him to do, how can I help him develop?

With preschool children they are naturally learning through emotions, visual images and play. In the early stages of a preschool child's brain development, learning letters, writing and logical thinking may not develop until they are 7 or 8 years old.
Always offer choices to preschool children; "Would you like me to read you a story, or would you like to play with your reading toys?" If a child is upset acknowledge that you see they are upset, "I see you are crying, can you tell me why?" If a preschool child is unable to tell you why they are upset, then redirect them by giving activity choices.

Question:
My grade school child is having difficulty reading, what can I do?

This is not an easy question to answer, there are many reasons why a grade school child may appear to be a slow learner. If a child has a learning difficulty such as dyslexia or a physical difficulty, such as eyesight problems; or a preference in hand, eye or brain hemisphere dominance, it may affect how a child learns; you may want to contact a professional to sort out any developmental issues.
My approach is not to define or label a learning difficulty but to present the methods shown in this book; my hope is they will work for you and your child, as they have worked for me and children in my care.

"A WALK IN THE JUNGLE" STORYBOOK
An activity story to improve a child's learning and development.

Some possibilities for children 2 years or older:
☺ Increased self-esteem.
☺ Increased self-control.
☺ Calms and relaxes children and adults.
☺ Creates a calm and relaxed environment.
☺ Makes changes in routine easier.
☺ Helps children be more self directing.
☺ Empowers parents and teachers to make a difference in their preschool child's growth.

A Walk In the Jungle is a storybook with a purpose.
The story includes activities and movements to help children and adults reduce daily stress; provide developmental movements; give children skills they will need to read and write; and above all have fun while playing.

The above lists some of the benefits the author has observed in himself and children under his care. The movements are adaptations from several personal development and stress reduction methods the author has experienced and used successfully with children over many years.

In an educational setting the black and white pictures can be copied and colored by children to provide a transitional or parent/child experience.

The story movements can be seen here:
https://howtoteachchildrentoread.ca/ and further on in this book in adult form pictures.
For ease of presentation to children, the storybook can be purchased at:
https://howtoteachchildrentoread.ca/_I used this storybook by folding it in half, showing the children the story picture, while I read the story and showed the children the story page movement.

 I cannot guarantee results by practicing any of the movement activities in this book.
The benefits listed above are purely anecdotal, based on observed results and benefits to myself and others in my care.
It is also interesting to note that after hearing the story about 6 times, children as young as 2 or 3 years old would read the story to their peers and show them the movements, purely from memory.

A WALK IN THE JUNGLE
A play-based preschool child development storybook.

Author: Paul Mackie

"Hi boys and girls, I am Nellie the elephant."

"Let's put on our listening ears."

LISTENING EARS

May help with: Listening and focusing skills.

How it is done: Grasp each ear with the thumb on the inside rim and the pointer finger on the outside rim; uncurl the ear down to the ear lobe using the pointer finger along with the thumb; bring pointer finger and thumb back to the top of the ear and repeat several times.

Nellie is waving at us with her trunk;

she wants us to join her for a walk in the jungle.

Put out your trunk and wave to Nellie.

Now wave with your other trunk.

ELEPHANT WAVE

May help with: Listening, balance and memory.

How it is done: Tilt your head, placing your ear on the shoulder while extending your arm forward; with your hand draw an infinity sign (an 8 on its side) the width of your shoulders, focusing your eyes beyond the fingertips. Your body and arm move as one unit with no twisting at the hips; do several times with each arm.

Nellie is going for a walk in the jungle, but the sun is so bright Nellie has to close her eyes.
Close your eyes;
let us be the sun.

What colour are you?
What shape are you?
How do you feel?
Are you cold or hot?

VISUALIZATION

May help with: Visualization and problem solving.

How it is done: Ask the children to close their eyes and imagine the sun as various colors, shapes and sizes.
Ask about feelings; remember, there are no wrong answers.

Nellie is getting thirsty because it is so hot;

she sees a cool clear pool of water and stops to take a drink.

Let's have a drink of water just like Nellie.

WATER

May help with: Learning and energy levels.

How it is done: Having a water bottle close by is an easy way to take a drink during the story.

Here comes one of Nellie's friends, Gordy the gorilla.

Look! Gordy is doing his gorilla talk.

Let's all do our gorilla talk.

Let's make some gorilla noises.

GORILLA TALK

May help with: Increased energy and relaxation.

How it is done: Place your hand on your neck (palm on the neck) with thumb on one side and fingers on the other; move your hand down until you feel your collarbone, jump over your collarbone and massage the soft spots between the next set of ribs and the collarbone; place your other hand on your belly button (do not massage with this hand); switch both hands and repeat for about 30 seconds.

Here come some monkey friends; see how they do the monkey walk.

Let's all do our monkey walk.

Let's make some monkey noises.

MONKEY WALK

May help with: Accessing the whole brain.

How it is done: Lift your left leg and touch your left knee with your right hand; put your left foot down and lift your right leg and touch your right knee with your left hand; repeat three or more times. Children having difficulty can match colored bands, gloves or stickers placed on opposite hands and knees.

There's Freddy the frog!
He's lying on a lily pad.

Let's all lie like Freddy on our lily pads.

Let's make some frog noises.

Let's do some frog jumping.

RESTING FROG

May help with: De-stressing, easier learning and whole body movement.

How it is done: Ask the children to lie on the floor, cross their feet at the ankles and give themselves a big hug by placing their hands under each arm pit.
Can be done sitting or lying down.

The heat is making Nellie tired;

look how she is yawning.

Let's all do a big elephant yawn just like Nellie.

ELEPHANT YAWN

May help with: Speaking and increased energy.

How it is done: Children take a deep breath and yawn; a yawning or elephant sound can be made.

Nellie wants to rest in the shade of some trees.

Let's all be trees and make some shade for Nellie.

Reach your branches up to the sky.

RESTING TREES

May help with: Visualization and imagination.

How it is done: Ask the children to stand up and imagine they are trees; put your arms straight up and spread your fingers wide.

You are all big strong trees, so reach up high, reach your branches to the sky;

now push your feet (your roots) hard into the ground;

reach high and push.

Here comes the wind!

Let's be the wind.

RESTING TREES

May help with: Relaxation and body control.

How it is done: With children standing, reach straight up as high as you can; spread your fingers (branches) wide and push your feet (roots) down to the ground; push and reach together; this puts the body into tension; sway like the wind from one foot to the other; this releases tension and leads to hopping; repeat several times.

Now it's getting dark.
Our branches are resting.

Let our branches hang down to the ground to rest.

RESTING TREES

May help with: Relaxation and calming children.

How it is done: Bend forward and let the arms hang loosely down to the ground.

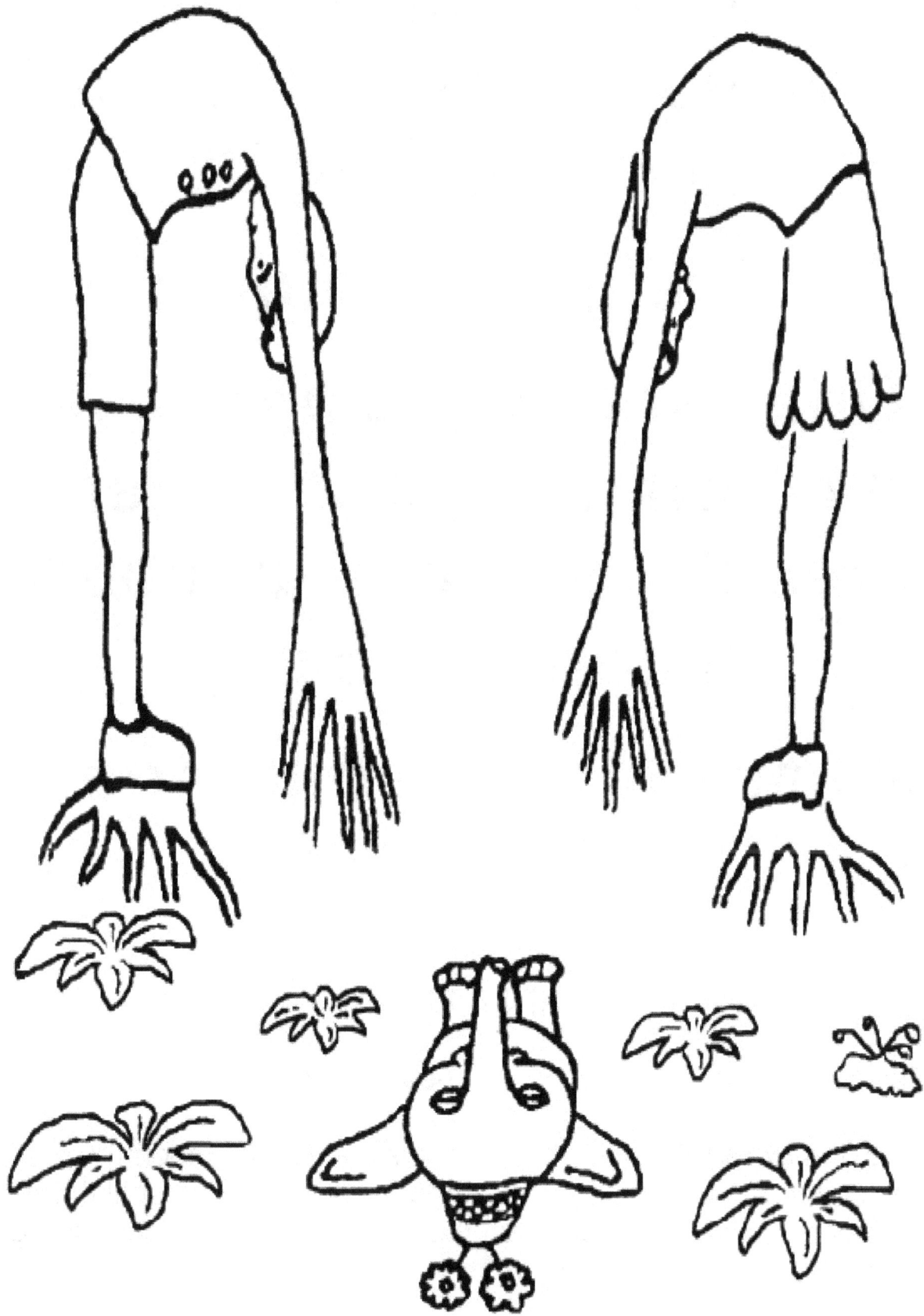

Close your eyes.
Nellie can see the bright moon coming up;

you are the moon.

Open your eyes and make a moon with your fingers; reach up high with your moon in the sky.

What shape is your moon?

VISUALIZE THE MOON

May help with: Visualization, shapes and communication.

How it is done: From the bending position form a moon by placing the tips of the fingers together; raise the arms until the hands are above the head, arch the back slightly and look through the circle formed by the fingers.

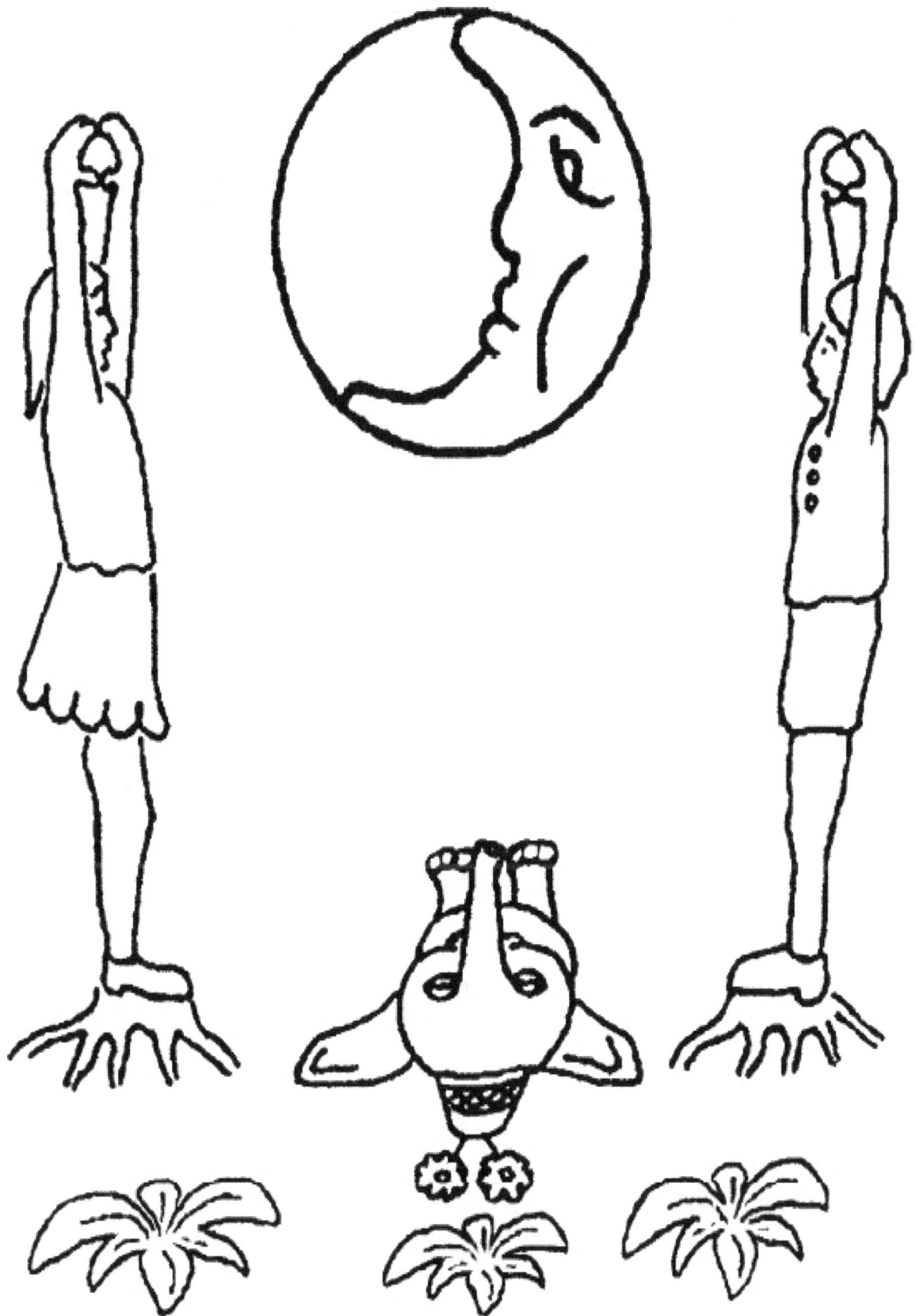

Here comes Sammy the snake; he is trying to sneak up on Nellie.

Let's all be ssssnakes. Wake up Nellie!

SNEAKY SNAKE

May help with: Posture, concentration and tension release.

How it is done: Resting on your elbows, lie face down on the floor; slightly arch your back by lifting your head backwards; relax by bringing your head down; repeat several times.

Here comes Leo the lion.

He's full of energy after his nap.

Let's all roar with Leo.

What other animals would we see in the jungle?

Let's be different animals. How would we move?

LEO THE LION ROAR

May help with: Energy and verbal expression.

How it is done: Put your fingers on your cheeks; find the pivotal points of the jaw by opening and closing the jaw; while opening and closing the jaw, massage the points with the fingers; a yawning or roaring lion sound can be made.

Well, boys and girls, it's time for Nellie to go back home.

Nellie says thank you; she had fun with you on her jungle walk.

Wave goodbye; goodbye Nellie!

See you tomorrow.

ELEPHANT WAVE

May help with: listening, balance and memory.

How it is done: Tilt your head, placing your ear on the shoulder while extending your arm forward; with your hand draw an infinity sign (an 8 on its side) the width of your shoulders, focusing your eyes beyond the fingertips. Your body and arm move as one unit with no twisting at the hips; do several times with each arm.

Ask the children to pick an animal from the "Walk In The Jungle" story; and to be that animal.

FREE EXPRESSION

As with all the movements the children are free to express themselves.
Usually the children will watch you and try to copy your movements.
With this page **you do not demonstrate,** instead you help the children talk about and act out animals of their choice.

The story closure: at this point transition the children to other activities by using an animal stamp (dollar stores usually have the ones that light up) or an animal puppet.

You can also transition the children to another activity by doing the Monkey Walk.

FOR THOSE THAT WANT TO KNOW MORE

LISTENING EARS
Why it is important: This activity has several purposes; it takes attention away from play and other activities while getting the children to focus and listen. This method may be used in kinesiology and acupressure to help with short term memory, listening and language skills. You can also use this to see if children are listening and transition them to another activity.

ELEPHANT WAVE
Why it is important: This movement acknowledges the children's presence in a friendly way and may help with listening comprehension, auditory memory, reading and sense of balance. Developing the ability to listen, retain information, cross the midline and have whole body co-ordination are essential skills for easy learning, reading and social interaction with peers.

VISUALIZATION
Why it is important: This helps children to use the right hemisphere of the brain (usually the creative side in most people). This activity teaches children how to solve problems by picturing what is going on in the mind's eye. It is best to use visualization images from the environment, or that children are familiar with. Being able to picture what is going on in the mind's eye is an important skill in problem solving.

WATER
Why it is important: Water assists learning and thought. Water helps us store and retrieve information, improves energy levels, improves mental and physical coordination. Water helps conduct the electrical and chemical processes of the brain for clear thinking.

GORILLA TALK
Why it is important: Being relaxed and energetic makes learning easier.
Massaging the kidney 27s pressure points increases energy levels, relaxes the body and helps both sides of the brain work together.

MONKEY WALK
Why it is important: Using both sides of the brain is essential for reading, comprehension and body coordination. This cross over movement activates both brain hemispheres simultaneously, increases whole body coordination, improves fitness and spatial awareness.

FOR THOSE THAT WANT TO KNOW MORE

RESTING FROG
Why it is important: Being relaxed and focused helps make learning easier and improves self-esteem. This cross over movement is helpful to de-stress the mind and body; increase attention; reduce negative thoughts and feelings; and may improve self-esteem.

ELEPHANT YAWN
Why it is important: Having more energy, a relaxed jaw and facial muscles makes it easier for children to communicate, sing and express themselves. Massage and yawning may increase energy; help with speaking; relax vision and clear thinking.

RESTING TREES
Why it is important: Being able to imagine and picture in the mind's eye is an essential problem solving skill. This movement uses visualization and imagination and teaches children how to tense and relax the body.

RESTING TREES
Why it is important: The movement teaches children how to use tension and release to gain body control and relax.

RESTING TREES
Why it is important: This movement calms and readies children for the next activity.

VISUALIZE THE MOON
Why it is important: Being able to imagine and picture in the mind's eye is an essential problem solving skill. Providing opportunities to express and verbalize such images is also beneficial.

SNEAKY SNAKE
Why it is important: After sitting for long periods, slightly arching the back helps release body tension, improve posture and concentration.
This movement helps relax body tension, increase hand-eye coordination and improve posture.

FOR THOSE THAT WANT TO KNOW MORE

LEO THE LION ROAR
Why it is important: A relaxed jaw and facial muscles make it easier for children to communicate and sing.
The roaring sound helps children express themselves; the same movement as the elephant yawn.

ELEPHANT WAVE
Why it is important: Developing the ability to cross the bodies midline, listen, retain information, and have whole body co-ordination, are essential skills for easy learning, reading, and good social interaction with peers.

STORYBOOK READER COMMENTS

"A Walk In The Jungle" has been a successful addition to our classrooms. It has been a wonderful and fun way to calm our children and ready them for daily transitions.
J White-Program Director.

"Gordy Visits The Mountains" has been extremely beneficial to my daughter's development. Being born with no binocular vision had a large impact on her gross motor development. My daughter loves to practice all the time with the gross motor equipment in this fun story setting. Now, six months later, her gross motor skills are right at age level and she's always excited to have the chance to practice her new-found skills on the equipment.
J White-Parent

Paul Mackie's remarkable book takes children through beneficial exercises in a fun and playful way. Children stay focused as they participate in each page of the story and can use their own imaginations as they follow the delightful story characters. What a great way for children to begin their day.
Rose Berzai-Parent

I use Paul's book in a home-based program with a six year old boy who is autistic. The boy laughs, enjoys himself, seems to be more focused and able to concentrate after the storybook exercises. Another good thing is that the exercises are transferable to different environments and can be done anywhere.
Emily Walsh-Special Education Assistant

"GORDY VISITS THE MOUNTAINS" STORYBOOK
Use movement to develop preschool children 2 - 6 years of age.

Studies and the works of some authors have shown that certain movements are a necessary part of a child's development for both mind and body (the balanced child). This book introduces some of those movements in a simple and play-based story.

The purpose of the book is to provide children up to the age of 6 years with a fun, creative movement activity that can become self-directing.

The benefits of the story can be improvements in:

♦ Social behavior.
♦ Physical coordination.
♦ Self-direction.
♦ Sequential processing (for reading and math).
♦ Creative child involvement.
♦ Making independent choices.
♦ Imagination.
♦ Self-esteem.
♦ Confidence, sensitivity, caring and sharing attitude.

It has been the author's experience to have children ask for this book in order to act out the story with their peers and friends; to see older children (of their own accord) use the story to instruct the younger children; to have children who are normally passive participate and express themselves; in other words, the story's benefits are the natural results of the children's own development.

It is the author's hope that you will use the stories "A Walk In The Jungle" and "Gordy Visits The Mountains" to prove for yourself that the benefits listed are achievable. If nothing else, above all, have FUN and play with your children!

Notes: Some of the activities in this storybook are the same as in the "Move and Improve Obstacle Course".

The "Gordy Visits The Mountains Story Mat" on page 129 shows you how to set up the obstacle course for preschool children.

"Gordy Visits The Mountains"
How to: use movement to develop a child

Hi! Boys and girls, my name is Gordy the gorilla. Let's put on our listening ears, just like Gordy!

LISTENING EARS

May help with: Listening and focusing skills.

How it is done: Grasp each ear with the thumb on the inside rim and the pointer finger on the outside rim; uncurl the ear down to the ear lobe using the pointer finger along with the thumb; bring pointer finger and thumb back to the top of the ear and repeat several times.

NOTE: It is OK if a child does not want to participate in an activity; however, that may indicate a problem for that child; just observe how they move and react to certain activities.

Today, Gordy is going to walk to his mountain friends for a visit.
Let's do some gorilla walking by hopping from one foot to the other, just like Gordy!

What other ways can we do some gorilla walking? What other ways can we jump and hop?

TWO FOOT HOP

May help with: Whole body coordination.

How it is done: Hop from one foot to the other with arms slightly out to the sides.
Ask children to show you other ways to hop; try not to prompt them.

Gordy comes to a flowing river.
Luckily there is a tree that has fallen across it.
Gordy balances slowly on the fallen tree to the other side of the river.
Let's all balance on the fallen tree and cross the river, just like Gordy!

BALANCE TREE

May help with: Balance, awareness of gravity and space.

How it is done: Walk slowly over the balance beam (a piece of sanded smooth wood 1"x 6"x48") by placing one foot in front of the other (heel to toe). Hold the hands of unsteady children if necessary; if the children are confident, then walk backwards.

Gordy steps off the tree onto some laughing rocks.
The laughing rocks start giggling as Gordy's feet tickle their heads, this makes Gordy laugh.
Let's all walk on the rocks and laugh, just like Gordy!
What other ways can we make people laugh?

THE LAUGHING ROCKS

May help with: Balance, feeling of laughter and joy.

How it is done: As the children walk on the rocks ask them to laugh.
Demonstrate by laughing yourself; be as natural as Possible.
Use joke books and funny situations.

Gordy sees a giant rock
with a big tunnel
hole through it.
Let's all crawl through the
tunnel rock,
just like Gordy!
What other ways
can we crawl?
What animals crawl?
Let's be a crawling animal.

CRAWLING TUNNEL

May help with: Using both sides of the brain together.

How it is done: The children crawl through a tunnel or under a table. Entice the children through by waiting on the other side of the tunnel (encouraging them to come to you); give lots of praise.

Gordy comes across another fallen tree on the path.
He swings both his arms and jumps over it with both feet.
Let's all jump over the fallen tree, just like Gordy!
What animals jump with two feet?
Let's be those animals and jump.

WHOLE BODY JUMP

May help with: Equal use of both sides of the body.

How it is done: Both arms and knees swing up together, as you raise your feet off the ground and move forward; The children jump over the balance tree.

Oh oh! Gordy steps on a thorn with his foot; look how he is hopping! Let's all hop on one foot, just like Gordy! What sort of noises would Gordy be making? How would he be feeling?

ONE FOOT HOP

May help with: Postural control of the whole body.

How it is done: Generally, toddlers will not be able to hop on one foot. To assist the children, have them hold onto the back of a chair and jump on one foot. Three to five year olds will be able to hop 3 to 10 hops; try hopscotch games.

Gordy sits down in a bed of flowers and removes the thorn from his foot. Sniff, sniff! Gordy smells the flowers. Let's smell the flowers, just like Gordy! What do the flowers smell like? What colors are they?

SMELLING FLOWERS

May help with: Developing the sense of smell; and can be calming and relaxing.

How it is done: Add a few drops of essential oil to some cotton balls or felt flowers and have the children guess the smell. Have pictures of the different smells to show children.

Here comes the rain to make the flowers grow; Gordy grows just like the flowers; he reaches up with his arms and pushes with his feet.
Let's all reach up with our arms, push with our feet, just like Gordy!
What other things grow?
Let's grow, just like them.

GROWING FLOWERS

May help with: Body control and relaxation.

How it is done: Have the children reach up with both arms then ask them to push with their feet (the feet should not rise off the floor, just like pushing a spike into the ground with your heel).

Here comes the wind; it blows Gordy around and around.

Let's spin around, just like Gordy! Let's be the wind. How would it blow?

SPINNING WIND

May help with: Balance and make learning easier.

How it is done: You spin both ways three times with your arms outstretched. For older children use a rotational balance board (two circular boards with a bearing between them that can spin as the child sits on it) or a rotational chair.

SAFETY TIP: Some children may be prone to seizures and should not spin or be spun around; always consult a doctor for children with special needs.
Spinning may reduce breathing and blood pressure, which may cause loss of consciousness.

The wind spins Gordy to his mountain friends; they are happy to see him. Gordy gives his mountain friends a big hug. Let's hug our friends, just like Gordy! What other ways do we greet or say hello to our friends?

MOUNTAIN HUG

May help with: Stress reduction and increased happiness.

How it is done: Ask the children to find someone to hug, or they can hug you. After reading the story a few times it is interesting to note that children will automatically find someone to hug as soon as you turn the page.

Gordy's mountain friends ask him to play balance ball.

Gordy stands on one leg and throws the bean bag at the target.

Let's balance and throw the bean bag, just like Gordy!

Can you throw the bean bag with your other hand?

BALANCE BALL

May help with: Body balance and hand/eye coordination.

How it is done: Stand on your right leg, throw the bean bag with your left hand; stand on your left leg, then throw the bean bag with right hand.

Here comes Gordy's friend Mickey the monkey; they are going to play balance catch. Let's play balance catch, just like Gordy and Mickey! Pass and catch with both hands.

BALANCE CATCH

May help with: Coordination skills and teamwork.

How it is done: Stand on one leg; throw the bean bag with one hand then the other hand; take turns throwing with each hand.

Gordy is using his gorilla talk to say goodbye. Let's use our gorilla talk and say goodbye, just like Gordy! Let's make some gorilla noises. Bye Gordy; bye-bye!

GORILLA TALK

May help with: Increased energy and relaxation.

How it is done: Place your hand on your neck (palm on the neck), with thumb on one side and fingers on the other; move your hand down until you feel your collarbone, jump over it and massage the soft spots between the next set of ribs and the collarbone; place your other hand on your belly button (do not massage with this hand); switch both hands and repeat for about 30 seconds.

FOR THOSE THAT WANT TO KNOW MORE

LISTENING EARS
Why it is important: Attention is taken away from play and other activities while getting children to focus and listen.

TWO FOOT HOP
Why it is important: Using both sides of the body at the same time, develops postural control and whole body coordination.

BALANCE TREE
Why it is important: Sequential movement may help with basic math, logic and reasoning skills. This movement helps the child develop an awareness of both sides of the body, gravity, space and balance.
Use of both brain hemispheres as well as the development of the vestibular system can make learning easier.

THE LAUGHING ROCKS
Why it is important: Balancing helps develop the vestibular system and balance, making it easier to learn. Laughter and joy promote a feeling of happiness and reduces stressful situations.

CRAWLING TUNNEL
Why it is important: This movement is a basic developmental stage which has a bilateral movement (the opposite arm and leg work together).
This leads to being able to use both sides of the brain together and can provide physical skills to help the child learn how to read and write.

WHOLE BODY JUMP
Why it is important: Jumping may help with equal use of the whole body, by lifting the whole body vertically off the ground.

ONE FOOT HOP
Why it is important: Hopping helps children gain postural control of the whole body; and awareness of the shift in gravity as the child moves.

SMELLING FLOWERS
Why it is important: A resting activity involving aromatherapy to develop the sense of smell; and to calm and relax.

FOR THOSE THAT WANT TO KNOW MORE

GROWING FLOWERS
Why it is important: The movement teaches the child how to use tension and release to gain body control and relax; in Chi Kung it is used to energize the mind and body.

SPINNING WIND
Why it is important: Spinning is said to improve children's learning abilities by moving fluid inside the inner ear, thus improving balance, coordination and the vestibular system.

MOUNTAIN HUG
Why it is important: Hugging is said to provide a sense of companionship and happiness, reduce stress, and improve quality of life.

BALANCE BALL
Why it is important: Balancing is said to develop learning through the vestibular and sensory systems. Throwing something at a target is said to develop a bigger brain.

BALANCE CATCH
Why it is important: Balancing and catching develop hand/eye and physical coordination skills. Working with a partner develops teamwork, self-direction and social skills.

GORILLA TALK
Why it is important: Massaging the kidney 27s pressure points is said to increase energy levels, relaxes the body and helps both sides of the brain work together.

NOTE: All benefits listed in this book are from benefits to the author and observation of benefits to children in the author's care.
The movements are adaptations from various movement modalities such as Yoga, Martial Arts, Kinesiology, Acupressure, Chi Kung etc.

TEACHING TIPS

This page offers suggestions for using the story to enhance each child's learning experience; by allowing each child the freedom to explore each creative movement, according to his or her own stage of development.

As the teacher: While reading the story, demonstrate each movement; allow each child to be creative, observing the child's movements and adjusting the level of difficulty to suit the child; end the story by giving the child an animal stamp and give lots of praise; above all, have fun!

Toddlers: Generally, are unsure of where they are in space; want to keep their feet safely on the ground; are learning to control their bodies; are afraid of gravity; and can generally only use one side of the brain at a time. With the toddler group, use a flat piece of non-slip material such as a rubberized painter's cloth, which works well when you draw the elements of the story on it (see "The Story Mat section). Lead the children through the story by showing the story picture and demonstrating each movement. As the children become more adept in their movements, introduce higher objects, which will then lift them higher off the ground; use the fallen tree as a balance beam, which is a piece of 1"x6"x48' wood sanded smooth; offer help to cross the beam by holding the child's hand lightly to steady the child and allowing them to learn by doing it themselves.

Listening ears: The ears are massaged from top to bottom with thumb and pointer finger. This may stimulate up to 400 acupressure points in the ear; younger children may not have the fine motor skills to do this movement but will attempt it.

Two-foot hop: This activity leads to a one-foot hop. The child uses imagination to become Gordy the gorilla as you hop from one foot to the other with arms down at both sides; while making gorilla noises.

Balance tree: This is a balance beam; you walk across it by placing one foot in front of the other, heel to toe; depending on the child's development.

The laughing rocks: Place the laughing rocks in various patterns and distances apart depending on the child's level of development; use felt faces for toddlers and "Flip Flop Faces" for older children; as you step on the rocks laugh; instruct the children to do the same.

TEACHING TIPS

Crawling tunnel: For toddlers, hold the tunnel steady and give lots of encouragement; always keep the child in sight.

Whole body jump: Both arms and knees swing up together, as you raise your feet off the ground and move forward; the child jumps over the balance tree.

One-foot hop: Generally, toddlers will not be able to hop on one foot; to help steady them, have them hold onto the back of a chair and jump on one foot; try hopscotch games.

Smelling Flowers: Add a few drops of essential oil to some cotton balls or felt flowers and have the children guess the smell; try to use smells that you have a picture of such as oranges and strawberries; which can also be used to help the child get to know the smell.

Growing flowers: Use a watering can to sprinkle imaginary water on the children as they reach and push their roots (feet) into the ground.

Spinning wind: You spin both ways three times with your arms outstretched. For older children use a rotational balance board (two circular boards with a bearing between them) or a chair that can spin as the child sits on it; ask the child to be the wind. **SAFETY TIP:** Some children may be prone to seizures and should not spin or be spun around.

Mountain hug: With this activity ask the children to find someone to hug, or they can hug you.

Balance ball: With this activity use a ball or beanbag and an ice cream pail as a target; demonstrate and then let the children decide when they are ready to do the activity.

Balance catch: Toddlers find it difficult to catch a moving object. To create success stand close to them and drop the beanbag in their hands. Give lots of praise, such as, "Great job! You caught it". A balloon can also be used to slow things down; balloons can burst, so be aware of choking hazards.

Gorilla talk: Demonstrate this movement by placing the thumb on one side of the neck and fingers on the other side; move the fingers down until you hit the collarbone, jump over the collarbone and massage the soft spots between the collarbone and the first set of ribs.

MATERIALS TO ENHANCE THE STORY

Story puppets: The story character, Gordy the gorilla, can be made in the form of a hand or finger puppet.

Animal stamps: Animal stamps can be bought at dollar stores.

Story telling cloth: A 5 foot x 13 foot painter's drop cloth sheet with the story drawn on the sheet; ideal for toddlers (see the Story Mat).

Balance tree: Make from a 1"x6"x48" for toddlers and a 2"x4" for older children and sand it smooth; draw on the tree with felt markers.
The leaves are cut from artificial green grass. The river in the story can be cut from an old shower curtain and attached to the wood with pins.

Laughing rocks: For toddlers cut 6" circles from felt and draw happy faces on them with a marker. Use a glue on rubberized backing material to create a non-slip surface.
For older children use "Flip Flop Faces" (a beanbag game from Discovery Toys).

Crawling tunnel: Can be bought from **https://howtoteachchildrentoread.ca/** cardboard boxes can be put end to end; or a table with a blanket over it.

Smelling flowers: Dollar store flowers can be set in a block of styrofoam; or use cotton balls; add a drop of essential oil with a smell of your choice.

Growing flowers: Use a plastic watering can, or large pail.

Spinning wind: Rotational balance boards (two circular boards with a bearing between them that can spin as the child sits on it); or a spinning chair.

Balance ball: Use small soft balls, or beanbags from dollar stores.

Balance catch: Use larger balls, balloons, Koosh balls or bean bags from most toy stores.

Note; Small objects can be choking hazards for pre-school children.

Lay out the story objects in the order that the story presents them.

Gordy Visits The Mountain Story Mat

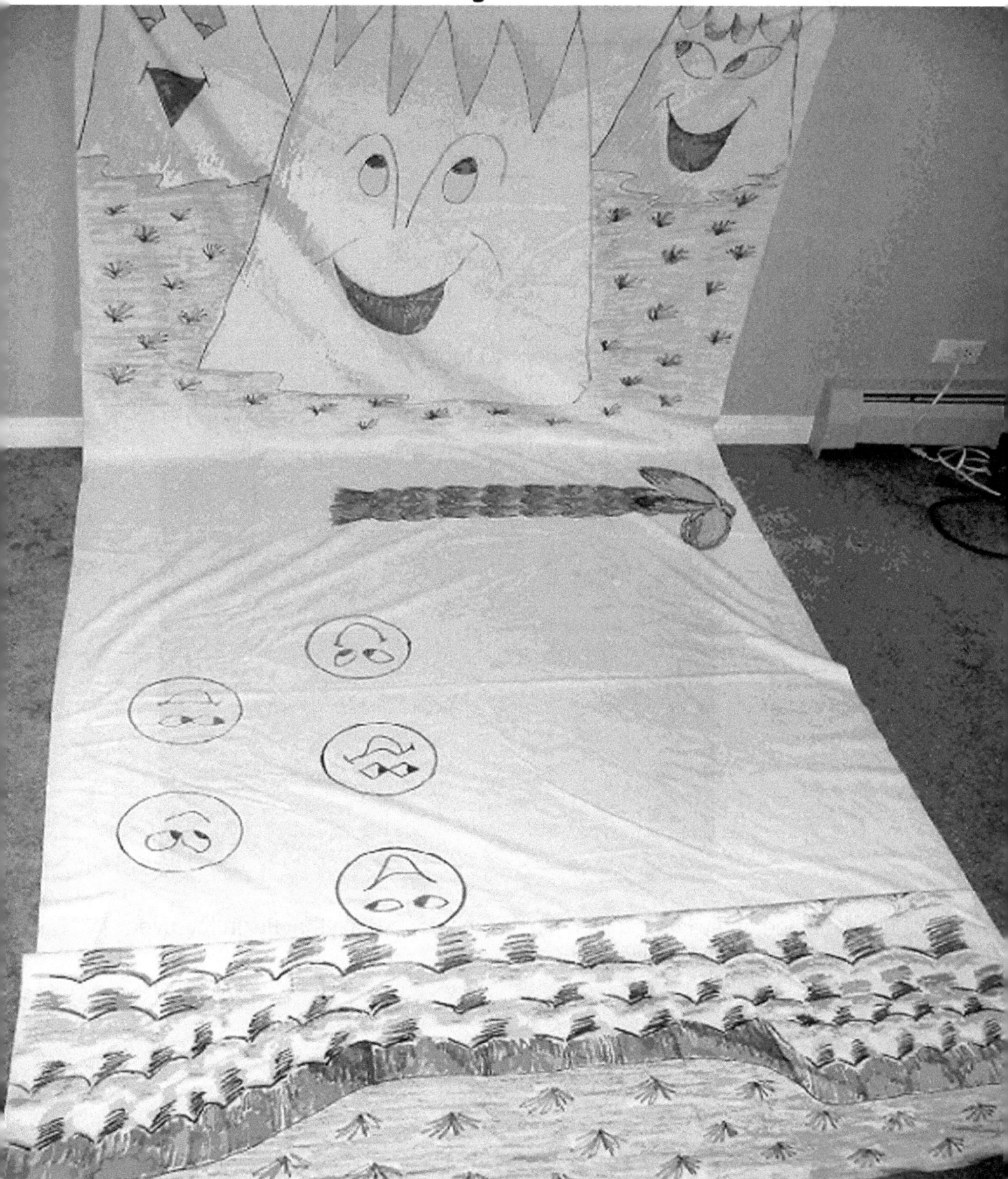

GORDY VISITS THE MOUNTAINS STORY MAT
"How to make the story mat"

The "Story Mat" follows the storybook "Gordy Visits The Mountains" storybook available from: https://howtoteachchildrentoread.ca/
The "Story Mat" can be made from any heavy material.
The one shown is a non-slip rubberized cotton type painter's drop cloth.
The size of the sheet can vary, depending on the floor space you have available.
The sheet you see in the pictures is 13 foot long by 4 foot wide and works well in most rooms.

Story sheet layout

mountains	tree	laughing rocks	river
4 foot long	2 foot long	4 foot long	3 foot long

4 foot wide x 13 foot long

The River: The river can be drawn on the sheet using colored felt tip pens. This is what it should look like:

I used a piece of "swimming fish" plastic shower curtain that fits in the river; this looks like fish in the river.

GORDY VISITS THE MOUNTAINS - STORY MAT

Crossing the River: A piece of 1"x6"x48" inch fir can be used as a palm tree.

The tree can be drawn on the sheet

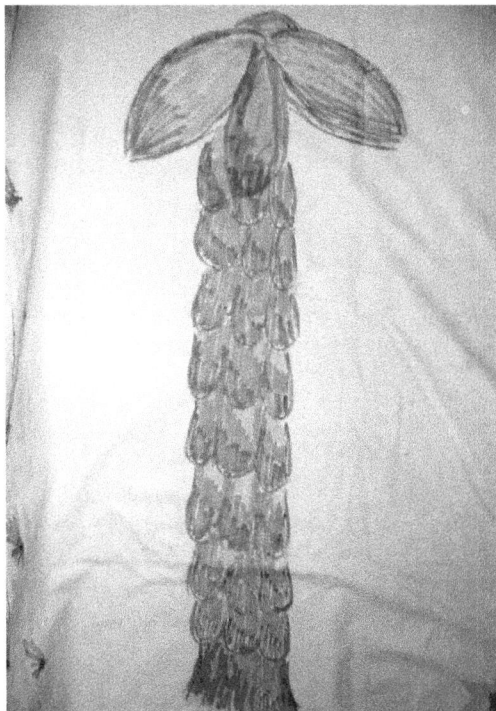

The tree can also be drawn on the wood, and some grass matting can be used for the leaves.

GORDY VISITS THE MOUNTAINS - STORY MAT

The Laughing Rocks: The rocks can be drawn on the sheet.

The laughing rocks can be bought as half circle, plastic flip flop faces from Discovery toys or Amazon; cut from 6 inch felt or cut from 1"x6" fir with the faces drawn on the wood.

Some rocks can have different expressions and there are 6 faces in all.

GORDY VISITS THE MOUNTAINS - STORY MAT

Balancing Tree: This is the same tree as the one crossing the river. The tree can be made of wood or drawn on the "Story Mat".

The Mountains: The mountains are drawn on the mat.

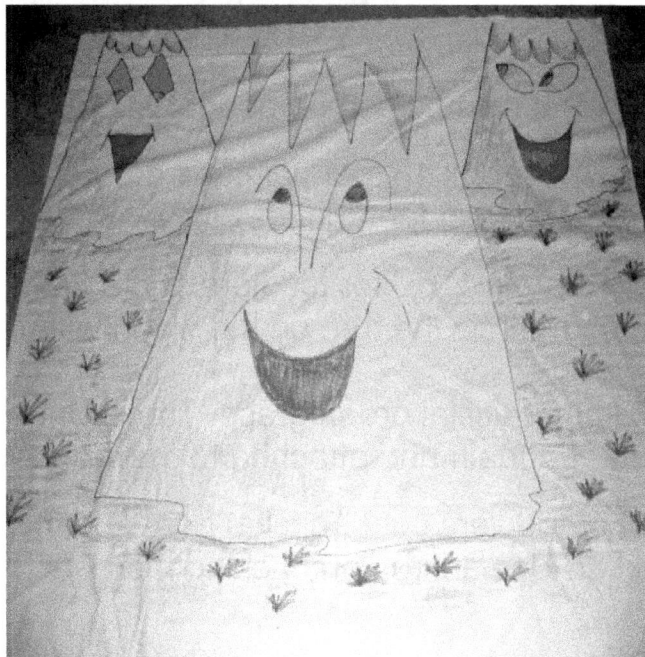

GORDY VISITS THE MOUNTAINS - STORY MAT

Materials to enhance the story

Story puppets: The story character Gordy the gorilla can be made in the form of a hand or finger puppet.

Animal stamps: Animal stamps can be bought at dollar stores.

Story telling cloth: A 4 foot x 13 foot painter's drop cloth sheet with the story drawn on the sheet (ideal for toddlers).

Balance tree: Make from a 1"x6" for toddlers and a 2"x4" for older children, sand it smooth, draw the tree on the wood with felt markers, and lacquer.
The leaves are cut from artificial green grass. The river in the story can be cut from an old shower curtain and attached to the wood with pins.

Laughing rocks: For toddlers cut 6" circles from felt and draw happy faces on them with a marker. Use an iron on backing material to create a non-slip surface.

For older children use "Flip Flop Faces" (a beanbag game from Discovery Toys), or plastic rocks from Amazon.

GORDY VISITS THE MOUNTAINS - STORY MAT

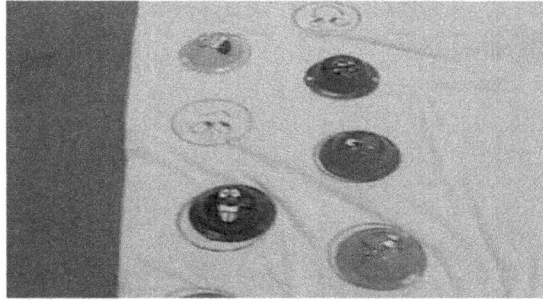

Crawling tunnel: Can be bought from Amazon; or large Cardboard boxes can be put end to end.

Smelling flowers: Dollar store flowers can be set in a block of Styrofoam, or use cotton balls; add a drop of essential oil of a smell of your choice.

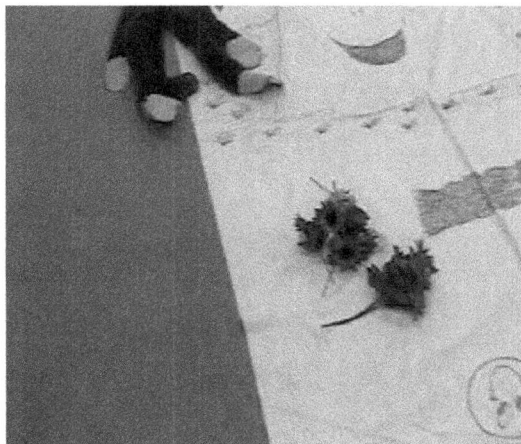

Growing flowers: Use a plastic watering can or large pail.

GORDY VISITS THE MOUNTAINS - STORY MAT

Spinning wind: Rotational balance boards (two circular boards with a Lazy Susan bearing between them); or a spinning chair.

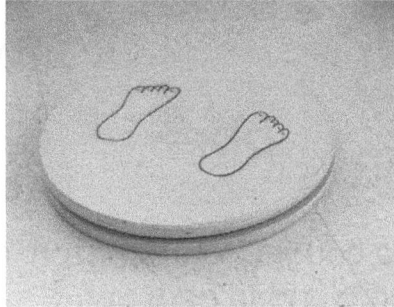

Balance ball: Use small soft balls or beanbags from dollar stores.

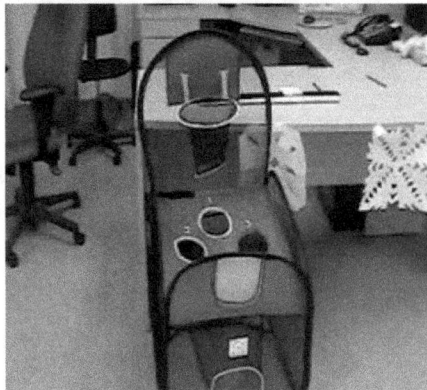

Balance catch: Use larger balls, balloons, Koosh balls, or bean bags from Amazon, or most toy stores.

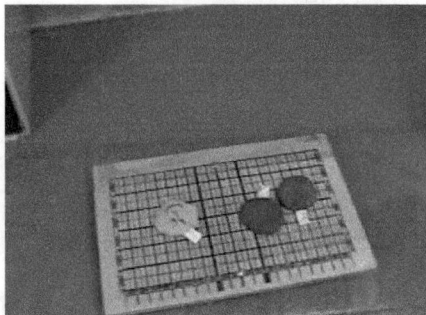

CHILDREN HAVING DIFFICULTIES READING SECTION

In this section I will present a series of activities and movements from the pre and grade school sections of this book.

At the end of this section is the "For Those That Want To Know More" section, which has a few stories that were memorable at the time they occurred; and showed me that movement and balance activities can make a difference in a child's development.

POSSIBLE OUTCOMES FOR GRADE SCHOOL CHILDREN

- Learn how to read and write.
- Develop the Brain's neural pathways.
- Better able to cross the midline of the body for reading and writing.
- Have better communication, increased cognition and thinking skills.
- Enhanced ability to sequence information.
- Increased ability to problem solve.
- Increased motivation.
- Increased organizational skills.
- Greater enthusiasm to learn.
- Improved coordination.
- Increase visual and auditory processing.

Outcomes are not guaranteed or proven results; the outcomes are observed results from personal use of the activities and observed results of children and adults in my care.

SET A GOAL AND BASELINE

From a parents perspective, your goal may be for your child to be the best that they can be, and to be able to perform well academically in reading, writing and other grade school challenges.

From your child's perspective, they may want to play better hockey, or score a goal in soccer, or achieve something in whatever they are interested in.

We will take the child's perspective and set a baseline and goal around something they are interested in.

WHAT CAN YOUR CHILD DO and WHAT DO THEY WANT TO DO?

How it is done: Ask your child to write a short sentence about something they would like to be better at; you may have to discuss this with them before they start.

Ask your child to close their eyes and think about what it is they would like to be better at.

Ask your child to open their eyes and tell you about what they saw and what they felt they needed to do better at; how did they feel emotionally?

Notes: Do not correct your child, even if their writing is scribble, or cannot be read; come up with a goal that would describe what it is they want to do better.

A measurable goal could be, "Score 2 goals in soccer or a hockey game." How many goals do they score now? The baseline is they currently may not score any goals; or they may want to "Score higher points on a video game." How many points do they score now, and how many do they want to score?
The point is to set a baseline and a goal they can notice, measure, achieve and move forward with.

To set a baseline, you can also use the Sideways Alphabet activity on page 145 to 147, and time how long it takes to do the activity; now we have a measurable baseline we will start with the Developmental Movements.

DRINK WATER

How it is done: Having a water bottle close by is an easy way to take a drink during the activity.

ENERGY BOOST

How it is done: Place your hand on your neck (palm on the neck) with thumb on one side and fingers on the other; move your hand down until you feel your collarbone, jump over it and massage the soft spots between the next set of ribs and the collarbone; place your other hand on your belly button (do not massage with this hand); switch both hands and repeat for about 30 seconds.

CROSSOVERS

How it is done: Lift your right leg and touch your right knee with your left hand; put your right foot down and lift your left leg and touch your left knee with your right hand; repeat, three or more times.

Participants having difficulty can match colored bands or stickers placed on opposite hands and knees.

How it is done: Ask your child to stand, or lie on the floor, cross their feet at the ankles and give themselves a big hug by placing their hands under each arm pit; can be done sitting or lying down.

SIDEWAYS 8

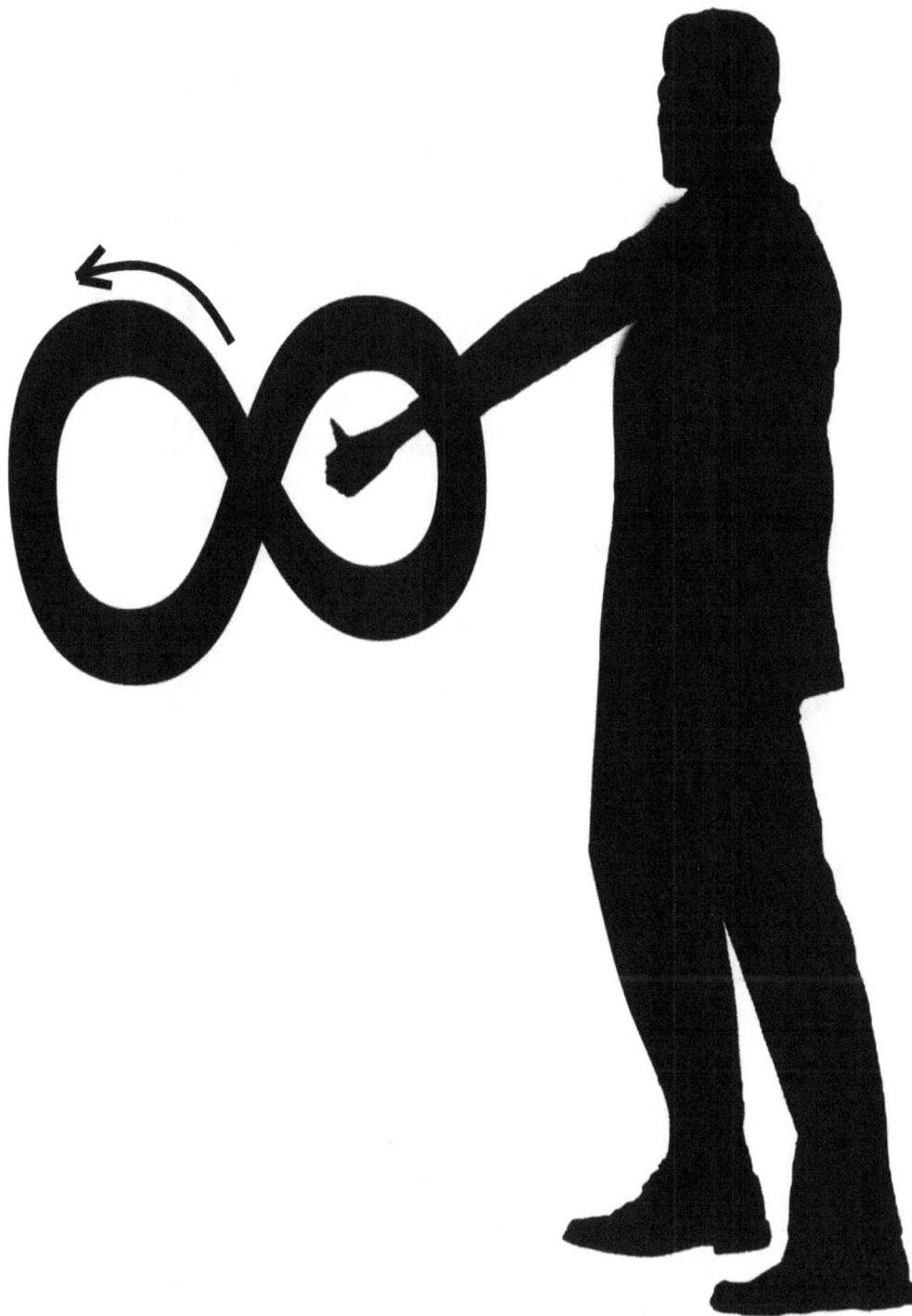

See instructions page 13.

See instructions page 14.

b
h
l
m
n
p
r

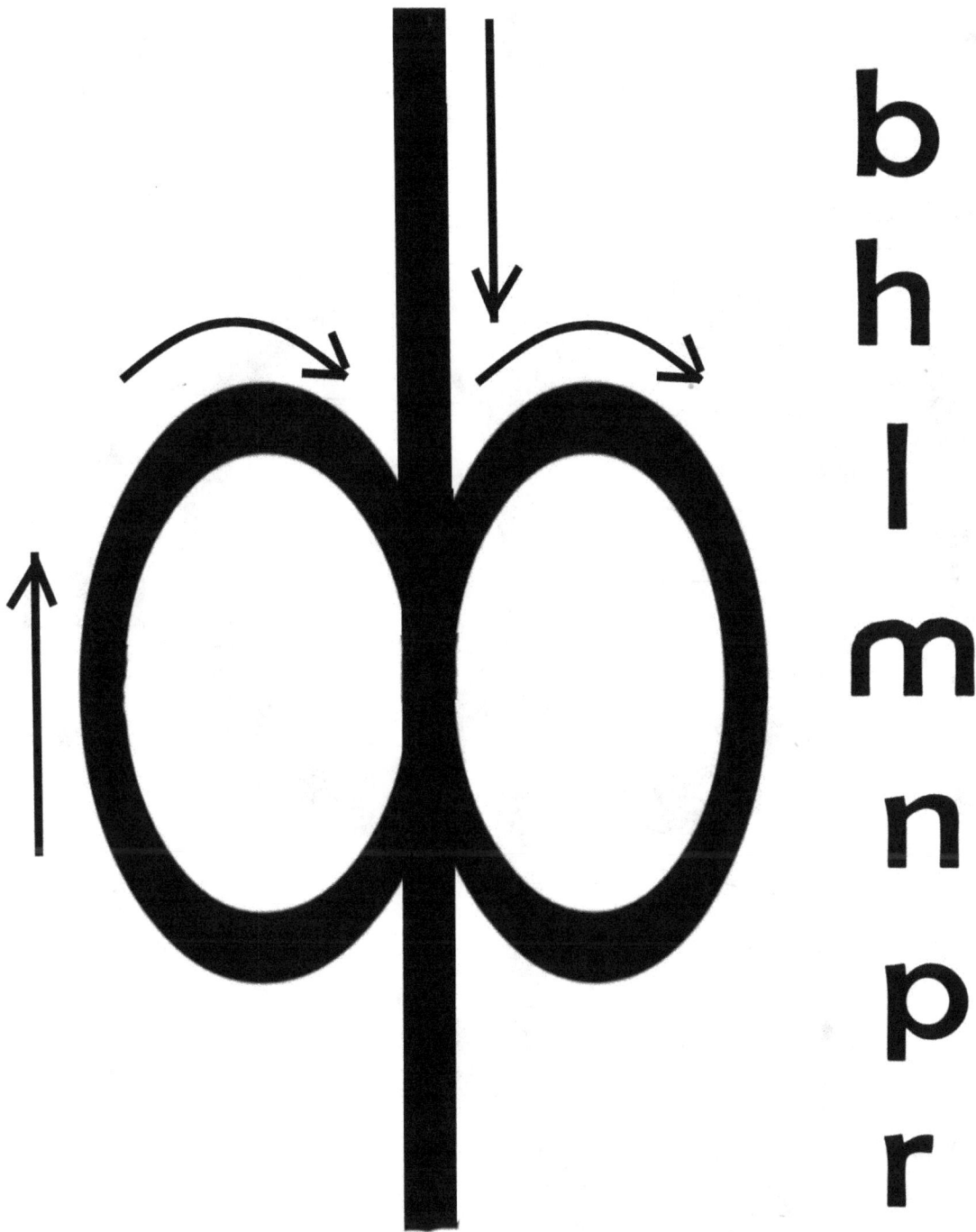

See instructions page 16.

a → b
c → h
d → l
g → m
J → n
o → p
q → r

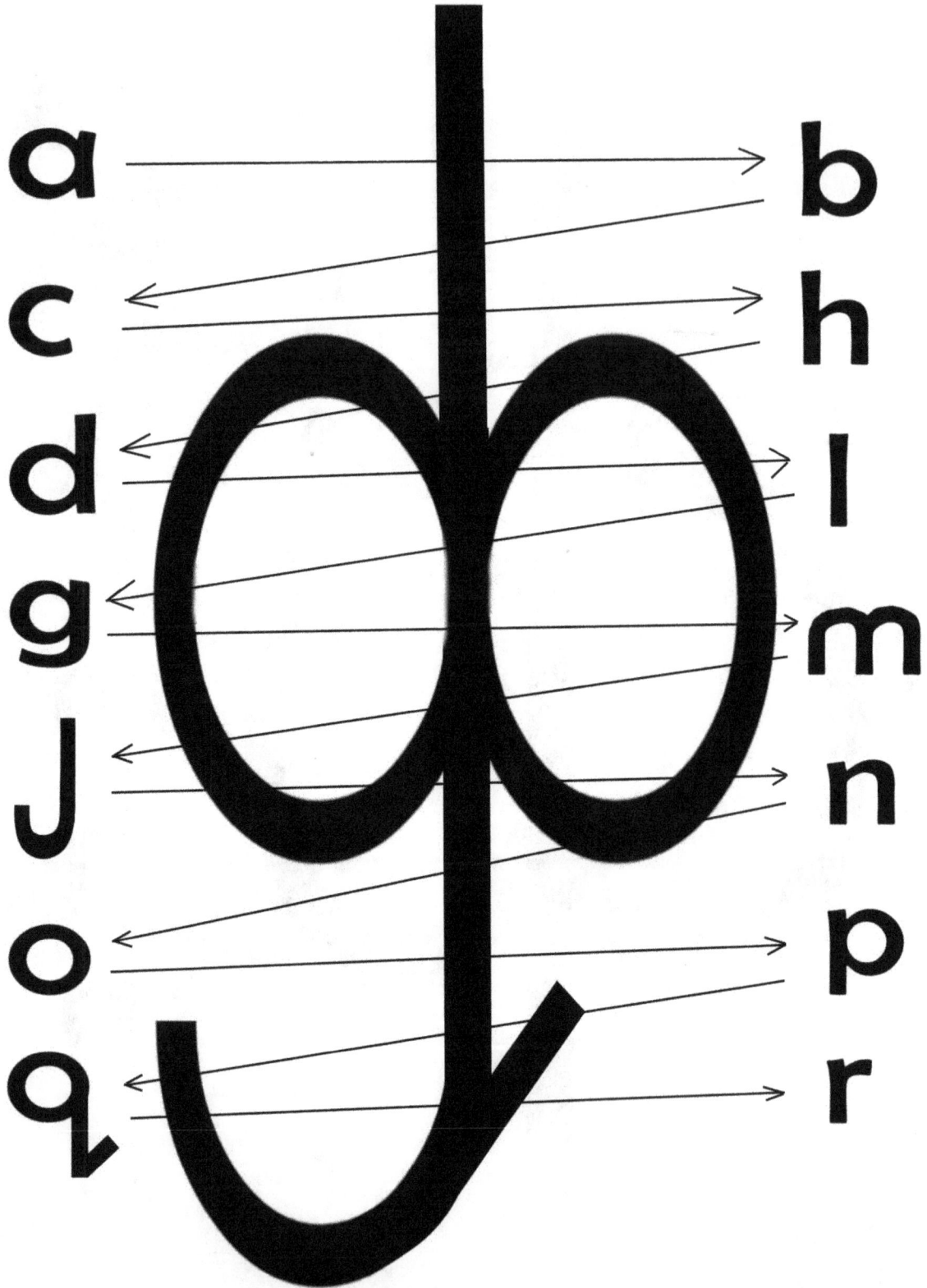

See instructions page 18.

CURSIVE ALPHABET WRITING

abcdef

ghijkl

mnopqr

stuvwxyz

See instructions page 20.

BALANCE BOARD WRITING

BALANCE BOARD SIDEWAYS 8
LEFT RIGHT AND CURSIVE ALPHABET WRITING

SIDEWAYS 8

LEFT ALPHABET

a c d g J o q

RIGHT ALPHABET

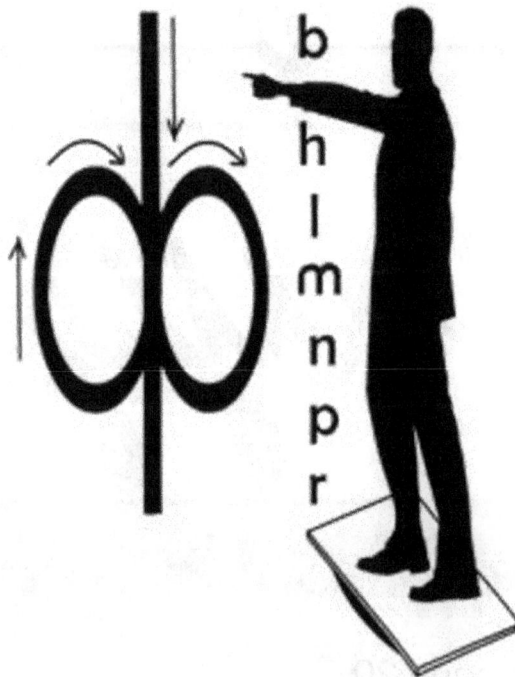

b
h
l
m
n
p
r

CURSIVE ALPHABET

abcdef
ghijkl
mnopqr
stuvwxyz

BALANCE BOARD PASS THE STICK

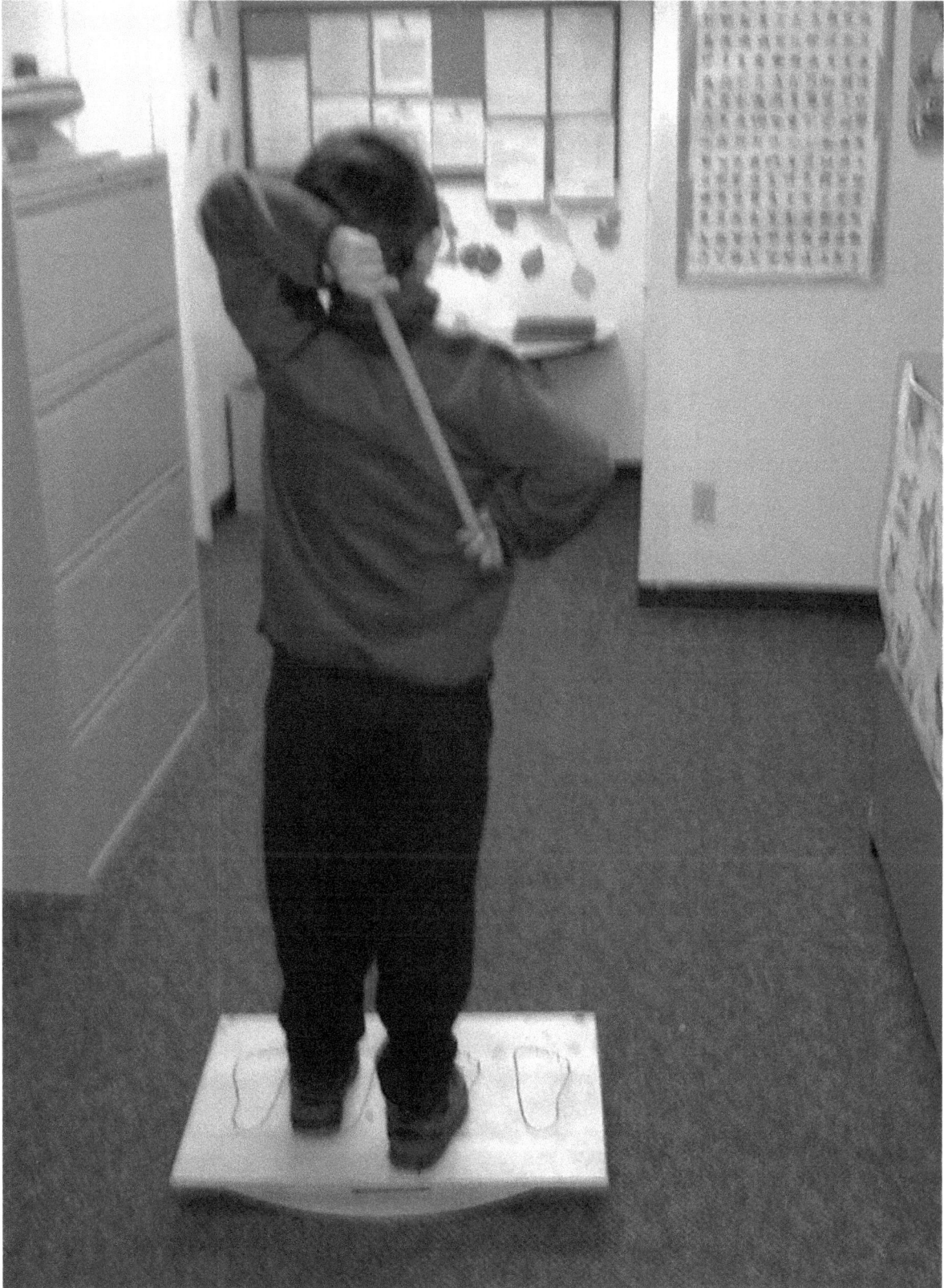

See instructions page 39.

BALANCE BOARD ACTIVITIES

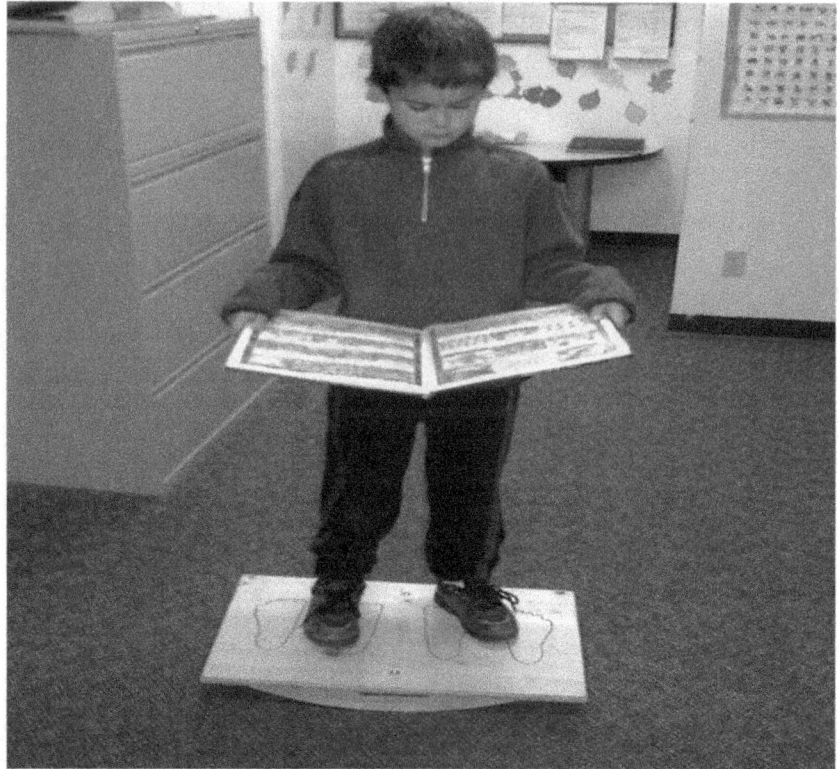

Read a book
on the
Balance Board.

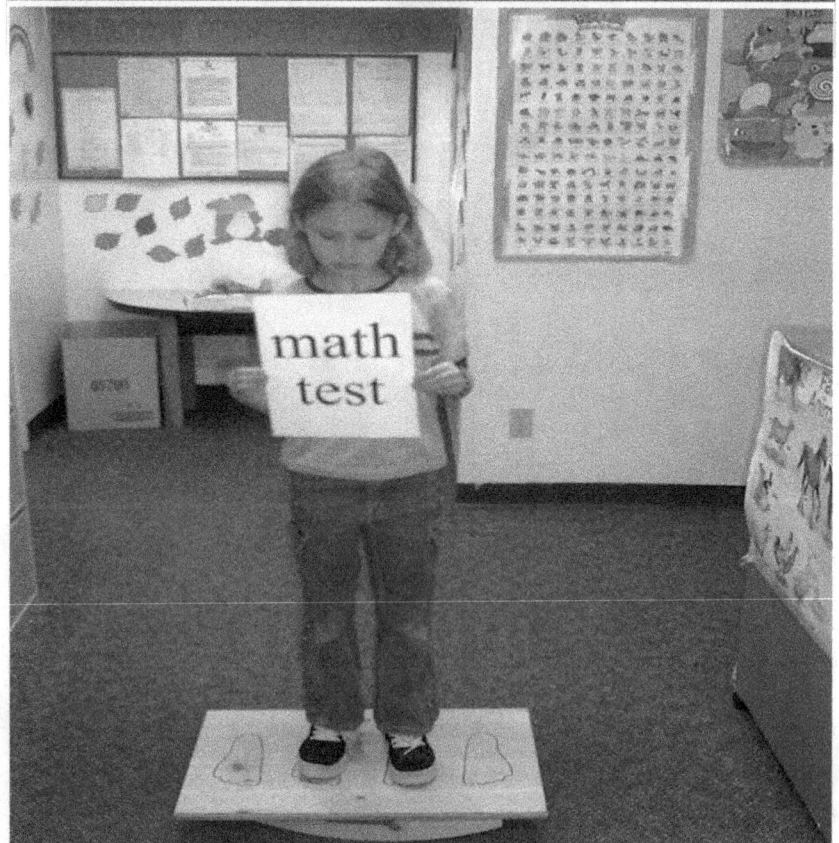

Practice a test
on the
Balance Board.

See instructions page 42 and 45.

OBSTACLE COURSE ACTIVITIES

walk heel to toe

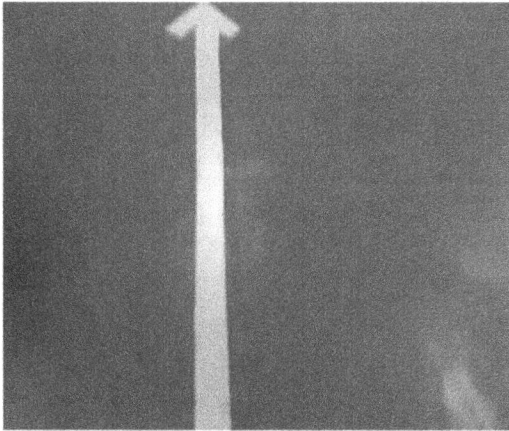

jump with two feet

hop left foot

crawl

hop right foot

balance on board

See instructions page 49 to 51.

HOW TO TEACH YOUR CHILD TO READ

THE METHOD: From the book "Fast Start For Early Readers Kindergarten": Start teaching your child the lowercase (short) sound of the English alphabet letters (phonemes – which are speech sounds); this involves "ear", "tongue", "eye" and "word building" training.

Step 1. Ear Training - Begin by slowly sounding out words of things you want your child to do: "Bring me a c-u-p." – "Show me something r-e-d." "c-l-a-p your hands." - "Bring me a p-e-n."

Step 2. Tongue Training – Sound out a word slowly "c-a-t," ask your child what sound they hear first and last; your child should say "c" and "t"; make sure your child pronounces the correct letter sounds.

Step 3. Eye Training – Start with "Fast Start For Early Readers Kindergarten" which teaches the Alphabet letter sounds in picture form (m, a, n, r, f, s, e, t, l, g, c, k, b, i, h, d, p, o, j, w, u, v, q, x, y and z); then vowels and blended consonants (digraphs).

Notes: The order in which the phonogram letter sounds are presented is based on the ease with which they are blended and able to be sounded out by children; it is not necessary for children to learn the letters in alphabetical order, or the names (long capital sound of the letters), as it may be confusing to learn the sounds and names of a letter at the same time.

With early readers it is best to keep things simple and step by step; for 2 and 3-year-old preschoolers keep lessons to one letter sound at a time and for a few minutes only; for 3 to 5 year old's this can be increased to 5 or 10 minutes; for fun, play based ways to teach your child to read see the book "Play Based Ways To Teach Your Child To Read" and "Fast Start For Early Readers Kindergarten" at http://howtoteachchildrentoread.ca

Step 4. Word Building Vowels and Consonants - Once your child can say all the short alphabet letter sounds go to the vowels and show how two consonants and a vowel create words; you could also teach the letter name or long sound of alphabet letters at this time.

Step 5. Word Building Digraphs - Digraphs are 2 or more letters forming one sound (a phoneme). Once a child has mastered the 26 Alphabet letter sounds, they are able to read most three letter words; once they master the most common letter blends (digraphs) they should be able to read most English written words.

Point to the first letter sound in the first picture word and say "m".

m_ _

Point to the first letter of the picture and ask, "What letter sound is this?"

m_ _

m_ _

If your child answers "m" correctly, point to the picture and say "mug".

mat
mop
mug

Point to the first letter sound in the first picture word and say "m" (all letters are lowercase short sound).

Point to the first letter of the picture and ask, "What letter sound is this?" If your child answers "m" correctly, point to the picture and say "mat".

Point to the first letter sound in the second picture word and say "m" (all letters are lowercase short sound).

Point to the first letter of the second picture and ask, "What letter sound is this?" If your child answers "m" correctly, point to the picture and say "mop".

Repeat the same process for the word "mug".

Your child should now recognize the letter sound "m".

Note: You are only teaching the first letter sound and not sounding or writing out the whole word.

All letters are lowercase or short letter sounds; we introduce capital long letter sounds and punctuation in other books by the author.

Notes: The preceding pages are samples from the book "Fast Start For Early Readers Kindergarten", which can be purchased at:
https://howtoteachchildrentoread.ca/

m _ _

m _ _

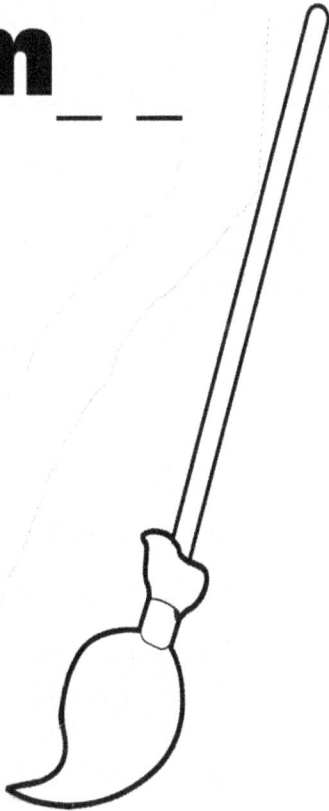

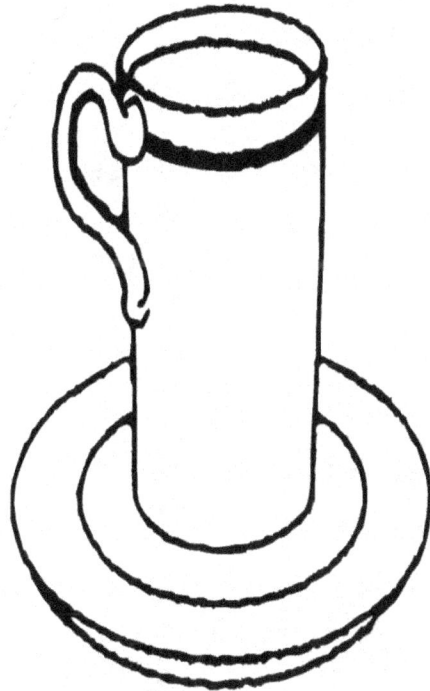

m _ _

FOR THOSE THAT WANT TO KNOW MORE

WHAT HAPPENS WHEN NOTHING SEEMS TO WORK?

The following is a story of how I started using the Balance Board with a troubled child and reached a point where I was about to give up the use of the Balance Board, when an amazing thing happened.

Several years ago, I was hired by a daycare to work with a three year old boy who had severe behavioral problems. As an Early Childhood Educator who had a lot of experience working with behaviorally challenged children I thought, "How bad could it be?" After all, he was only three years old.

Tommy (not his real name) knew a lot of words; he favored "F _ _ _ You!" followed by a string of two to three word sentences of the same language. At first, I tried the usual methods of behavioral management such as time-out, transitional methods (timers, communication of changes in activities etc.), rewards and praise for good behavior, but all to no avail. It was at this point that I decided to use a new approach, new to me anyway; this was to use a great piece of equipment called a Balance Board.

The techniques of the Balance Board Program which I knew did not fit with this situation, so I decided to change the method into a play-based routine.

I introduced Tommy to the Rotational Balance Board.
I started by taking Tommy to the staff room, which was large, open and free of distractions. At first, I just sat on the Balance Board and spun around a few times; then I asked Tommy to do the same. Tommy tried it, quickly got bored, and then started jumping on the staff room furniture and pulling pictures off the walls. I persevered.

With all this spinning I would get dizzy. Tommy found this to be funny and would stop his negative behaviors to come over and laugh at me! I would hold my head, groaning, and tell him I felt sick. It became a game for Tommy, giving me a clue about how to reach him.

Tommy started using the board. The first thing I noticed was that Tommy did not get dizzy; he would spin for five minutes, get up off the board and walk away (I later found out this could be a possible indicator that a person may have sensory difficulties). Another thing was his awareness of where he was in space; he would run his hand along the wall all the time (another possible indicator of sensory difficulties) and would slide on his back on the floor, bumping his head quite hard on walls, doors and furniture.

FOR THOSE THAT WANT TO KNOW MORE

When Tommy was used to the daily routine of five minutes on the rotational board, I introduced the Rocking Balance Board. The method for the use of this board is to stand perfectly balanced (adjustable rockers can increase the level of balance difficulty) while carrying out certain hand/eye coordination activities (hitting targets or catching balls).

I had Tommy stand on the Rocking Balance Board and throw a soft bean bag at my stomach.
Whenever he would hit my stomach dead-on, I would bend over and say, "Ow! that hurt." If he missed and hit some other part of my body I would not react as much; the more I reacted, the more he hit the target and the louder he would laugh.

Tommy's behaviors had decreased a little and he was swearing less, but after two months, I began to doubt whether the balance board activities were having much effect. It was at this point that an amazing thing happened.

One day after our usual five minutes of spinning Tommy stood up and said, "I feel dizzy;" something had changed, which was not amazing in itself; the truly amazing thing happened the next day.

The next day I was watching as a boy took Tommy's train set; I quickly stepped in to prevent Tommy from snatching back the train and hitting the boy as he typically would do. To my surprise, Tommy came over to me and said, "He has taken my train!" I asked Tommy, "What should we do about that?" Tommy replied, "He took my train set. Let's go and ask for it back!" (twelve words, in sentences – truly amazing for this little boy). I helped Tommy get the train back by using his words.

From that point on, Tommy's use of vocabulary increased dramatically. He could communicate his needs and feelings and his violent outbursts decreased. Tommy still had behaviors, but more at the level of a developing three year old.

Another interesting thing was that Tommy stopped running his hands on the walls, although he would still slide on the floor; he would however slow down and gently touch his head to objects instead of hitting them hard.

FOR THOSE THAT WANT TO KNOW MORE

MY CHILD SEEMS TO BE A SLOW LEARNER WHAT CAN I DO?

A concerned parent who brought her child (Billy, not his real name) into the after school care program asked me the above question; I decide to help by using some of the developmental techniques I had used on other children.

When I work with children of any age, I usually find out what they are interested in and then choose a course of action. The parents goal for her child was for him to come up to the developmental level of his classroom peers; the child's goal was completely different.

I asked Billy what the problem was, he said, "I can't score any goals in soccer". With any parent or child's goal it is best to set a baseline, so you have a point of reference, to see if there are any improvements.
I asked Billy to close his eyes and imagine he was playing soccer; I then asked him to describe what was happening. Billy said he was kicking the ball, but it would always go to the left or right of the goal.

For this 6 year old I used some of the activities in the storybooks "A Walk In The Jungle" and "Gordy Visits The Mountains"; using the "Crossovers", Balance Beam, eye teaming exercises and some sequential movements. After the movement activities, I asked Billy to close his eyes and imagine he was playing soccer and to kick the ball, I asked him where the ball was going, he replied, "The ball is going into the goal's net." About a week later I asked Billy's mom how he was doing, she replied, "Great, he is scoring more goals and his class work is improving.

CAN YOU HELP ME WITH MY SPELLING?

An 8 year old child Mary (not her real name) who was in the after school program asked me if I could help her with her spelling list; I asked Mary to show me her spelling list; I read the list of 20 words and asked her to spell them; she got 5 right.
I decide to use a combination of developmental movements, the Balance Board and visualization activities.

I asked Mary to drink some water, do Listening Ears, Energy Boost, Crossovers and Connections; then I asked Mary to stand on the Balance Board and sound out each spelling word on her spelling list; then to look at the spelling list, close her eyes and imagine and see the words on the page; I asked Mary to step off the Balance Board; I then read each spelling word and had Mary spell out each word; she got all 20 correct.
The next day I asked Mary how she did with the spelling test at school, she replied, "I got all 20 right".

FOR THOSE THAT WANT TO KNOW MORE

IS THERE ANYTHING YOU CAN DO FOR MY AUTISTIC CHILD?

I was working as a Teacher's Assistant in a Junior High school, when a parent asked me if I could help his teenage autistic son John (not his real name), as he was not doing well at school and seemed to be living in a world where he would act out TV shows that he had watched on TV the night before; and would not talk very much. I observed the child during classes; he would do what the teachers asked of him; saying nothing.

With this child I decided to use some of the "Move and Improve" activities and take him to the gymnasium to use the Balance Beam and walk the lines of the basketball court. I also used a technique called "The Calf Pump" mentioned in the book "Smart Moves" by Carla Hannaford; Carla suggests this movement is related to shortened calf muscles, toe walking (walking on tip toes) and the inability to speak.

John did improve, he stopped acting out TV shows; appeared to be in the present moment with no toe walking. However, John did start to speak in class, by refusing to do certain lessons and telling the teachers what he wanted to do instead; a somewhat normal response for a teenager.

DEVELOPMENT IS NOT ALWAYS WHAT YOU EXPECT.

I was working as a Community Care worker in a day program for difficult to work with special needs adults. One of my clients, Jeff (not his real name) a 33 year old, 250 pound adult man who spoke only a few words, was toilet trained, walked on his tip toes, usually did as he was asked to do and appeared to have the physical and cognitive abilities of a 3 year old.

For this client, we went to local playgrounds and used the swings, merry go rounds, walked on rocks, irregular surfaces and climbed steep hills.

Over a few months Jeff started resisting doing some activities, started walking flat footed and at home would pee himself while sitting on the couch. Unfortunately, Jeff's parents pulled him from the day program, saying he was resisting doing things he normally did at home like using the toilet and going to bed when asked.

This was an unusual result, but my observation was that Jeff was growing, developing a sense of self and making his own choices. It is common for a 3 to 5 year old to use toileting habits as a way of gaining control and it is possible the flat footedness was indicative of lengthened calf muscles, due to climbing steep hills. The results appeared negative but may have well been a developmental stage for this person.

With Ontario leading the way, the Council of Ministers of Education endorses play-based learning

The Council of Ministers of Education believes that purposeful, play-based early learning sets the stage for future learning, health, and well-being. In the Council of Ministers of Education Statement on Play-Based Learning (2012), the council describes the benefits of play, as recognized by the scientific community, early learning experts, and children and families alike.

Learning through play is supported by science

* Scientific evidence demonstrates that neural pathways in the brains of children are built through the exploration, thinking, problem solving, and language expression that occur during play.

Learning through play is supported by experts

* Experts such as Lev Vygotsky identify play as a leading source of social, emotional, physical, language, and cognitive development. Intentional play-based learning allows children to investigate, ask questions, solve problems, and engage in critical thinking.

Learning through play is supported by children and families

* Children themselves are naturally driven to play, and early learning through play often takes the form of manipulating objects, acting out roles, and experimenting with different materials.
* Parents also understand that play is valuable to development, allowing children to construct, challenge, and expand their understanding of the world around them.

OTHER BOOKS BY THE AUTHOR

https://www.amazon.com/author/paulmackie
https://howtoteachchildrentoread.ca/

	A WALK IN THE JUNGLE - Storybook Prepare preschool children emotionally, intellectually and physically, before they go to grade school. Give your child an unprecedented, LIFELONG advantage, simply by reading them a storybook; a storybook UNLIKE ANY OTHER you've seen before. It feels so good to see your child achieve milestones, absorb knowledge like a sponge and develop a true love of learning.
	GORDY VISITS THE MOUTAINS - Storybook Gordy Visits The Mountains helps children develop physical coordination; improves self-direction; enhances decision making; and promotes problem solving. A fun play-based child development storybook activity gets your child ready to learn.
	LEO LEARNS TO READ - Storybook Leo Learns To Read shows you how to teach the fundamentals of reading This storybook helps children learn the fundamental keys to reading, and gives children the exciting gift, that they are "Reading to Learn".
	ALPHABET PARK -Storybook This story is designed to teach children the basics of reading; so, they will learn to read, and then "read to learn". Each page has a story about a letter of the alphabet; then there is either a question about the story, or a movement activity; children are asked to write the sound of the alphabet letter.

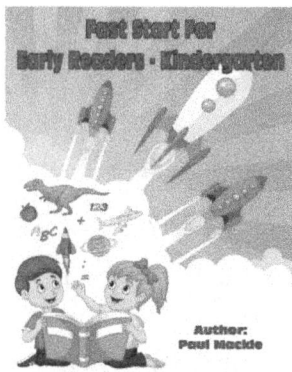	**FAST START FOR EARLY READERS KINDERGARTEN** This book introduces preschool children to the Alphabet letter sounds in picture form; children quickly and easily learn to read most three letter words. This book shows you how to develop your child's "ear", "tongue", "eye" and "word building" skills, so that your child will quickly be able to read most three letter words.
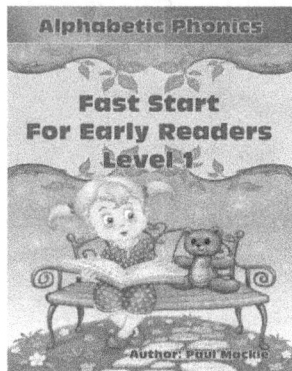	**FAST START FOR EARLY READERS LEVEL 1** This book introduces short sentences using the phonetic sounds of the alphabet and pre primer sight words. The book has large easy to read letters and matching black and white pictures to help preschool children easily learn to read.
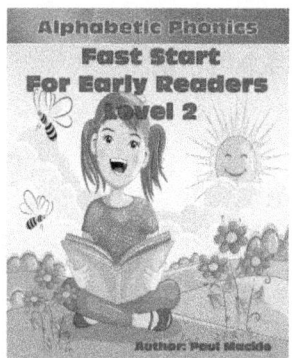	**FAST START FOR EARLY READERS LEVEL 2** With this book children learn how to read four or more word punctuated sentences; recognize 26 letter sounds of the alphabet; as well as 92 Pre-Primer Sight Words.
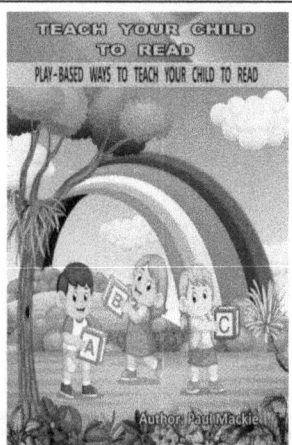	**PLAY-BASED WAYS TO TEACH YOUR CHILD TO READ** This book shows you: What play based toys and learning to read materials to use; A step by step plan to teach your child to read and write; How to present learning to read materials to your child; How to present learning to write materials to your child; That learning to read and write can be fun and play-based; How to set up the in-home reading and writing environment; That pre-school children can learn to read and write.

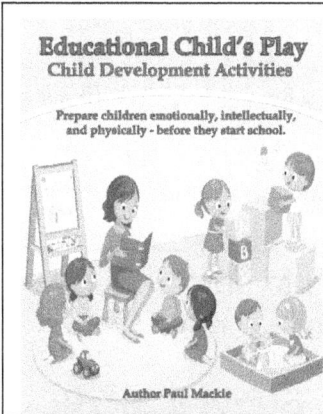	**EDUCATIONAL CHILD'S PLAY** Play Based Child Development Activities. Prepare pre-school children emotionally, intellectually and physically, before they start school. A book jammed packed with play based child development activities.
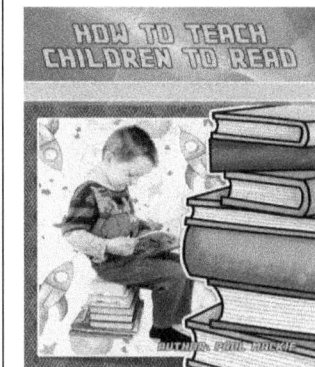	**HOW TO TEACH CHILDREN TO READ** This book introduces children to 86 phonetic sounds of the English language with a step by step plan to teach a child of any age how to read. How To Teach Children To Read also introduces the 220 Dolch word list (sight words) so that a child will be able to read, write and spell most written words.
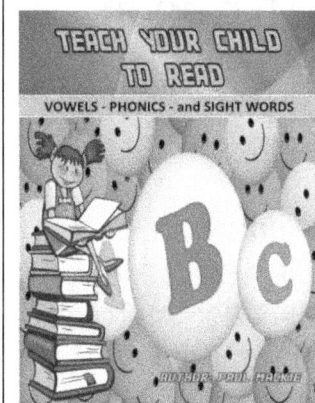	**TEACH YOUR CHILD TO READ – VOWELS - PHONICS and SIGHT WORDS** *This book* teaches 60 blended phonetic sounds; the 220 Dolch Sight or Whole Word list; and how to read three, four or more letter words.
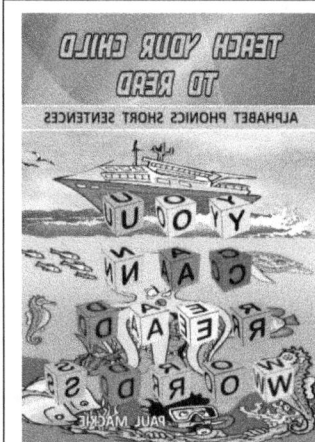	**TEACH YOUR CHILD TO READ – ALPHABET PHONICS – SHORT ENTENCES** This book is for parents and people with little or no teaching experience; and is presented in an easy to follow play-based method that any child can follow. Teach your child to read alphabet letter phonic sounds in short sentences, by sounding out short three and four-letter word sentences. Books 1 and 2 teach the alphabet sounds, vowels and Sight Words; this book puts that knowledge into practice.

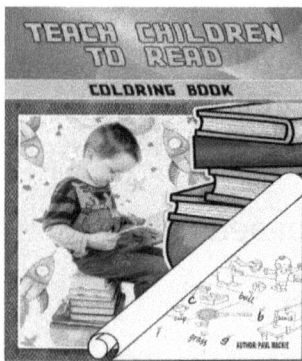

TEACH YOUR CHILD TO READ COLORING BOOK

This book is a coloring book with a combination of coloring book pages from How To Teach Children To Read, Alphabet Park and other activities that introduce children to the Alphabet letter sounds (phonics) and sight words needed to be able to read and write most English written words.

PRE SCHOOL COLORING AND PUZZLE BOOK

This coloring book is designed to help pre-school children with the following possible benefits: increase creativity; a free time activity; a transitional activity; a soothing distraction; improve fine motor skills; calm and center the mind; stimulate the brain and the senses; help focus the mind in the moment: and take the mind off distracting thoughts.

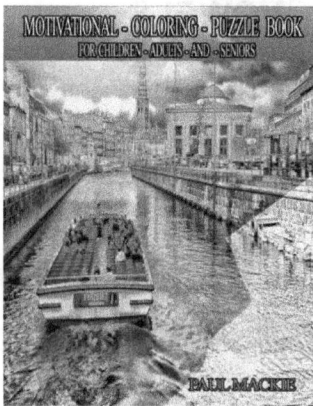

MOTIVATIONAL COLORING PUZZLE BOOK

This book has inspirational pictures, comic art, and puzzles for children, adults and seniors. It is the author's hope that readers may experience some of the following benefits: Give children a calming activity; help children learn to read and write; increase creativity; challenge thinking skills; reduce stress; improve state of wellness; improve fine motor skills; calm and center the mind in the moment.

ADULT AND CHILDREN COLORING BOOK

A 128 page adult and children coloring and puzzle book. The pictures and puzzles are printable for any age group, from adult coloring to children. This book was designed for my 42 year old daughter who had a stroke and has limited movement and communication due to her stroke. This book is helping her use both hands; improve her fine motor skills; and improve logical thinking skills.

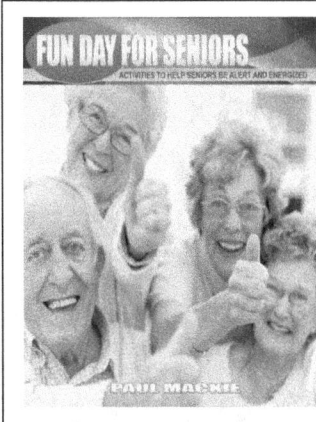

FUN DAY FOR SENIORS
Thousands of activities to help seniors be alert, in the moment, energized and living a full life.

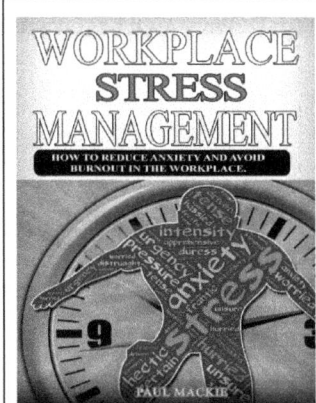

WORKPLACE STRESS MANAGEMENT
Do you feel stressed and anxious at work?
You're about to discover easy to do workplace stress management activities to reduce stress, anxiety, and the possibility of a nervous breakdown in the workplace.
You will Learn: a 5-minute exercise to start and finish your day; practical, easy to learn movements to help reduce workplace stress.

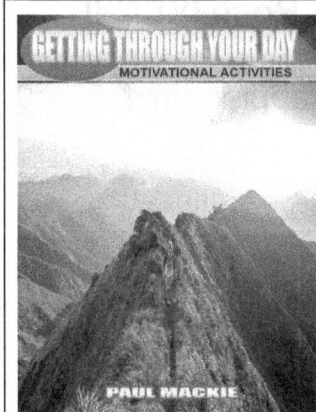

GETTING THROUGH YOUR DAY
Getting Through Your Day- Motivational Activities to help you reduce stress, be alert, in the moment, energized, and living a full life. This book introduces you to a 5-minute movement based exercise to start your day. You will learn to focus the mind, energize the body and be ready for a meaningful day.

BIBLIOGRAPHY

Smart Moves by Carla Hannaford, Ph.D. ISBN 0-915556-26-X
Why learning is not all in the head.

Creative Play for the Developing Child by Clare Cherry. ISBN-0-8224-1632-8
A book that illuminates the value of play in relation to child development during the first few years of life.

Is the Left Brain Always Right? by Clare Cherry. ISBN-0-8224-3911-5
A guide to whole brain development. This book demonstrates the need for educational programs that develop the whole child. It also shows you how to create appropriate activities and learning opportunities.

Creative Movement for the Developing Child
by Clare Cherry. ISBN-0-8224-1660-3
A book to develop sensory perception during the various stages of a child's growth.

Aromatherapy Workbook by Marcel Lavabre ISBN-0-89281-346-6
A book that explores why and how to use aromatic oils.

Fundamentals Guidebook by Gordon Dryden & Colin Rose ISBN-0-905553-44-6
Part of an educational kit of activities to raise a brighter happier child.

Kindergarten Maximum Stimulation by Lyelle Palmer
A book by researchers to improve young children's learning abilities.

The Hug Therapy Book: by Kathleen Keating
Explains the positive results of how and why you should hug.

The Throwing Madonna by Dr. William Calvin
Dr. Calvin puts forward the theory that throwing and running on large rocks led humans to develop bigger brains.

Ontario Early Years Framework
http://www.edu.gov.on.ca/childcare/OntarioEarlyYear.pdf

ABOUT THE AUTHOR

The author (Paul Mackie) is married, has 4 children, and 6 grandchildren; and lives in Calgary, Alberta, Canada.

Paul has over twenty years of experience working with children and adults as an educator, and personal care worker.

Paul is a certified Early Childhood Educator in British Columbia, and a level two Early Childhood educator in Alberta Canada.

Paul has worked as a Community Care worker with special needs children, adults and seniors; and has worked with children in Daycares, Day Programs, and the School System.

Paul has had several careers, with certification as a Marine Engineer; Industrial Millwright, Welder; Early Childhood Educator; with experience as a Teacher's Assistant; Special Needs Childcare Worker; Brain Gym Instructor; Senior Building Manager; with courses of study such as "The writing Road to Reading", "Accelerated Learning" and other Brain development courses.

Paul is now retired; his last working position was as Senior Building Manager for a non-profit housing society.

Visit: http://howtoteachchildrentoread.ca/

Please feel free to leave a book review on Amazon or Contact me at: educationalchildsplay@gmail.com

Have a great day.

Paul Mackie
The Child Development Guy

Questions contact: educationalchildsplay@gmail.com